The Sports
Factory

The Sports Factory

AN INVESTIGATION INTO COLLEGE SPORTS

Joseph Durso

AND

The New York Times Sports Department

QUADRANGLE/The New York Times Book Co.

Portions of this book appeared in *The New York Times* in a different form.

Library of Congress Cataloging in Publication Data

Durso, Joseph
   The sports factory.

   Includes index.
     1. College sports. I. New York Times. Sports
Dept. II Title.
GV583.D87   796   74-24285
ISBN 0-8129-0533-4

To the members of the Class of 1975
—and beyond

Contents

Foreword

In January of 1974, a small army of people was assembled in a conference room at *The New York Times* by James Tuite, the paper's new sports editor. They were there to exchange thoughts on one of the great issues of the day in sports, one that did not show up in box scores or "game stories," nor even for that matter in sports reports from behind the scenes: the scouting, recruiting, and paying of high-school athletes by the colleges.

The agenda for the caucus consisted of that one item because Tuite, a onetime high-school football end who had *not* been heavily recruited or subsidized, was anxious to find out what—besides home runs, touchdowns, homestretch sprints, field goals, and Howard Cosell—made the sports world tick. A glance at the sports pages most days provided the answer: money. And, by the mid-1970s, it was clear that people around the world had the leisure time and money to spice their lives with more and more sports, either as participants or customers or armchair viewers.

Consequently, the sports pages had begun to resemble the front pages and financial pages, because money had long since been supplying sports with the resources and opportunities of business. It had also been supplying them with such headaches of business as antitrust actions, tax problems, contract disputes, hassles between agents and management, city-hopping, league-jumping, franchise-switching, Congressional investigations, and strikes by players, umpires, parimutuel clerks, and jockeys.

It did not take too much imagination, or suspicion, to relate this state of affairs to most of the changes that had revolutionized sports, particularly professional sports, since World War II. But not much searching had been done in the world of amateur sports. However, by the beginning of 1974, the vibrations were widening: college football teams had just collected half a million dollars in some cases for appearing in the bowl games on New Year's Day; the stampede for the basketball tournaments was under way; the number of colleges being punished by the National Collegiate Athletic Association for violating the amateur code had increased; other colleges were abandoning varsity sports because they were becoming too expensive; and still others, desperate to keep pace, were reaching down to the junior high schools with expressions of interest in 6-foot-8-inch teen-agers.

By the time Tuite's "team" had finished exchanging thoughts on this situation, the decision was made to take a closer look. So a dozen sports writers were detached from their regular assignments for varying periods of time and were banded into a task force whose task was to cast a spotlight on college recruiting.

During the next two months, they traveled from Los Angeles to Raleigh-Durham, from Notre Dame to South Shore High School in Brooklyn, from N.C.A.A. headquarters in Kansas to the ghettos in the Bronx where boys bounced basketballs in the playgrounds. They interviewed university presidents, athletic directors, head coaches, ex-coaches, and ex-quarterbacks; recruiters and recruited (the "hunters and the hunted"); famous alumni and not-so-famous alumni; chemistry majors, football majors, and even Johnny Majors; and celebrities from Dean Rusk to Col. Frank Borman, the astronaut.

From their search, the writers learned that not much had changed since Rutgers defeated Princeton in the first college football game a century earlier—or since Lafayette traveled to West Virginia at the turn of the century, played a football game there, and returned home with favorable impressions of West Virginia's big tackle. (Two weeks later, the big tackle was playing for Lafayette.)

But if the "system" had remained essentially the same, they also learned, the pressures within it had continued to grow with the arrival of the "tramp athlete," football bowl games, basketball, the paid recruiter, the jet airplane, and television. Nobody was against winning a ball game or even a championship, as such; but the most important thing, as they saw it, was to weigh the values of the entire educational system against the rewards that the varsity teams might offer.

The enduring nature of the problem, in fact, could be seen in two landmark reports separated by nearly half a century. In 1929 the Carnegie Foundation for the Advancement of Teaching issued its massive study *American College Athletics*, in which it warned that the time had come to stop the excesses in the sports system. In 1974 a similar warning was issued in a report to the American Council on Education by a group headed by George H. Hanford, after a study sponsored by the Carnegie Corporation of New York and the Ford Foundation. Excerpts from both reports appear in the following pages, along with the findings of the *Times* team.

These findings were printed in *The New York Times* in a series of articles over a six-day period in March, 1974, and since then in numerous stories and letters of reaction. They represented the work of Neil Amdur, Steve Cady, Gerald Eskenazi, Sam Goldaper, Robin Herman, Arthur Kaminsky, Leonard Koppett, Arthur Pincus, Jay Searcy, William N. Wallace, and Gordon S. White, in addition to the author of this book. All are sports writers on the *Times* who worked under the overall direction of James Tuite and Harold Claassen, assistant sports editor, and under the immediate direction of Steve Cady and Joe Durso. Messrs. Cady, Eskenazi, and Pincus also were especially helpful in the preparation of this book.

Their report in the *Times* ran to about 20,000 words, with the encouragement and guidance of A. M. Rosenthal, managing editor of the Times, and Seymour Topping, assistant managing editor, who also served as the chief critic and devil's advocate of the team's operations.

The investigation was monitored, at a respectful distance, by Jonathan Segal, editor, and Roger Jellinek, editor-in-chief, of Quadrangle/The New York Times Book Company. It was at their behest, and with their help, that the findings were radically expanded into this volume, in the belief that all of us might learn something about the values and directions of sports in American education.

The Sports
Factory

CHAPTER I

Bear Bryant's Air Force

At the stroke of noon, Bear Bryant's Air Force was revved up and ready to go. The first sortie would be flown by the three full-time pilots attached to headquarters, the Athletic Department of the University of Alabama. Two of the pilots would be manning the lead plane, a turboprop reserved for the chief, Paul Bryant, the sixty-year-old head coach of football and director of all athletic operations. The radius of action: half a dozen states across the southeastern United States. The supporting forces: ten recruiters stationed at strategic spots en route.

Mission: Signing Day in the South.

It was a day like no other, the second Saturday in December, a day when the air was still filled with the echoes of the autumn's activity on the college campuses. A day when 150 of the region's finest, strongest, quickest schoolboys would sign college contracts —to play football.

By the time Bryant's air strike was under way, a mood of dedication and purpose had long since gripped people from Gainesville, Florida, and Baton Rouge, Louisiana, on the lower perimeter, to Lexington, Kentucky, on the upper rim. In between, a mood of expectation settled on seven other cities, all of which ranked as rival headquarters in the day's business.

They were Nashville and Knoxville in Tennessee, Oxford and Starkville in Mississippi, Athens in Georgia, and Auburn and Tuscaloosa in Bear Bryant's Alabama. Forces in those cities did not all have his airpower, but they all had his aim. And from their flagstaffs, they flew the names of the warring parties: the University of Kentucky, Vanderbilt, the University of Tennessee, the University of Mississippi, Mississippi State, Auburn, the University of Georgia, Louisiana State, and the University of Florida. They were all members of the Southeastern Conference, and this was the day of decision.

By mid-afternoon, telephone lines were tied up at the ten command posts—the athletic offices on each campus—with townspeople and newspaper people clamoring for the vital statistics. Newspapers in seven states were preparing to print complete lists of the victories of each of the colleges: the recruits won for the next four, or maybe even five, years. Television and radio crews were covering the airports, college walks, and private homes. And all over the South, whole communities were girding for the great annual invasion.

Bear Bryant had started the day on the Tuscaloosa campus by greeting two recruits, who with their parents had driven in from out of state to be signed. One of them was a high-school All-American lineman named Larry Kennedy, whose father was a professor at Mississippi State. But if blood was thicker than water, something else was thicker than either, and the army of recruiters knew better than anyone else what that was.

By 12:30 in the afternoon, Bryant was in Columbus, Georgia, to sign a tackle named Mike Sebastian. He beat forty other colleges to the prize. At 3:30, he was in Tampa, Florida, to sign a linebacker named Dewey Mitchell. "I don't sign many," Bear said, pausing to issue a sort of communiqué, "but I see a lot. I sign the ones that think it's important."

One of the future members of the college Class of 1978 who

Paul (Bear) Bryant, head football coach at the University of Alabama and chief of the South's highest flying recruiters, carries the message to the people.

thought it was important to be signed personally by Coach Bryant was Mike Sebastian. He hadn't been able to make up his mind which college to choose. But after Alabama advised him that Bryant would honor him as the first signee of Signing Day, he naturally chose Alabama.

"I don't like the idea of chasing and pampering a boy, and I don't do it," Bryant protested, while chasing and pampering Mike Sebastian. "But I used to, when I was younger. I'm not going to baby and beg and pet and give a boy that kind of treatment, because he's sure not to be treated that way when he gets to Alabama."

Having divested himself of any "softness" on the matter, he nonetheless made a beeline for the Sebastian home while 150 other football coaches, student assistants, team trainers, and recruiters from other colleges pursued different targets across the South. Like Bear Bryant, many used private planes and pilots. Others made it by car, and still others had taken the precaution of stationing themselves at the right place at the right time.

"Some recruiters will baby-sit with an outstanding boy for a week or more before Signing Day," reported Clem Gryska, the deputy to Bryant and his full-time recruiter at Alabama. "They do it to avoid possible interception by rival recruiters. They see them at breakfast, check on them at school, after school, and then go by their homes at night.

"To many people, it's like a postseason game. If Auburn signs twenty and Alabama signs nineteen, Auburn wins the game."

In Columbus, the mother of Mike Sebastian was fussing around the house as though Henry Kissinger were expected for lunch.

"We were all real excited that he was actually coming to our house," she remembered later, meaning Bryant, not Kissinger. "We all chipped in and cleaned house on Friday. And I made a cake and some sandwiches and things, and we had people in."

The people included three high-school coaches, Mike's girl friend, a television cameraman, some neighbors, two newspaper reporters, a photographer, a lawyer, and an alumnus of the University of Alabama. The signing took place in the living room, and when it was over Coach Bryant hugged Mrs. Sebastian, who exuded: "I got a picture of it." She got two pictures, in fact. One was hung in the family's den, and the other was placed in Mrs. Sebastian's billfold.

The deed was done, and it was celebrated at an elaborate buffet luncheon that the Sebastians had spread for the twenty-five guests. It was noted, though, that Coach Bryant—apparently under the pressure of the long day of zooming around the countryside—ate only one apple. When he left the happy scene and pointed his Air Force toward the next target, one of Mike's brothers retrieved the apple core and showed it off to his friends like a relic. A relic of one of the most significant days in American higher education.

"It's the apple that Bear Bryant ate," he announced proudly.

Butch Lee came home from basketball practice at DeWitt Clinton High School in the Bronx, pried open the mailbox on the ground floor of the rundown apartment building at Eighth Avenue and 153rd Street, poked inside to make certain that he hadn't missed anything, glanced at the peeling walls in the lobby, and shook his head. "Three more today," he said.

He walked up the five flights of stairs, went into the bare little apartment, and turned on the light dangling from a socket. On top of a wooden dresser was a Dewar's White Label carton overflowing with college brochures. Under his cot were three shoe boxes stuffed with 300 letters. They contained offers to attend colleges— at seventeen, Alfred Lee was the most heavily recruited guard in America.

"Here they are," he said, sounding a little battle-weary. "I don't mind it. But it's funny sometimes. If I tell a recruiter I'm interested in mathematics, he tells me, oh, they have a great math department. I tell another recruiter I'm interested in business, and they tell me how good their business department is. No matter what it is that I want to major in, their schools have the best departments."

The commotion started, he recalled, after he had scored fifty points in a basketball game at a summer camp in Pennsylvania, a showcase for the hot shooters in high-school circles. That's when the phone began to ring and the mailbox began to fill up with letters and brochures.

"I guess the two things I'm looking for is the academic and the basketball," Butch Lee said, trying to keep his head while all about him were losing theirs.

"English," he added, "is my most best subject."

Sandy Climan sat down on the steps of the Harvard campus and reflected on the joys of his exalted rank at the age of seventeen: he was an "All-American" math wizard, was valedictorian of his class of 850 a few months earlier at the Bronx High School of Science, was a finalist in the Westinghouse talent search, and had Scholastic Aptitude Test scores that averaged 750, which placed him in the top 1 percent of the more than a million students who had taken the exams.

He also was editor-in-chief of his school's yearbook and of its *Math Bulletin*; he knocked down a grade of 100 in an advanced-placement test in calculus; and he conducted an independent research project that discovered a new bovine brain compound capable of leading to a better understanding of degenerative brain disease. He was, said the assistant principal of his school with understatement, "A very unusual boy."

But when Sandy Climan sat down this day to ponder his success, he wondered about people's values in such things. To get him into Harvard and to keep him there at about $6,000 a year, his father and mother both stuck to their jobs, skipped vacations, and curtailed their style of living. His prizes and national scholarship awards added up to only about $1,900, and they covered only his freshman year.

One of the problems—maybe the critical problem—was that

Sandy was only 5-feet-6. The only team he had ever performed with at the Bronx High School of Science was the debating team.

"A couple of times," he said, focusing on his rags-to-rags success, "I was ready to say 'Buy me' to interviewers from top colleges. I didn't want to be a financial burden on my parents. But nobody offered me any money."

Senator Robert C. Byrd, Democrat of West Virginia, turned aside from such grave affairs of the day as foreign policy, inflation, and the Middle East situation, and glanced at the speech he had prepared for delivery on the floor of the United States Senate.

"It is time," he read, "that athletics were viewed in a more proper perspective. It is time we all realized that few things are less vital to our national survival than a fall without N.F.L. football, the outcome of a single baseball game, or the location where high-school athletes choose to continue their athletic training.

"The overemphasis has come step by step, bit by bit, and will continue until it reaches some undetermined point in the future. It might prove the wiser course, then, for the N.C.A.A. to remove all sanctions on recruiting, scholarships, and 'expense money,' and require only that schools make public the total costs of their athletic programs—even the expenses now hidden because they go for unethical and improper activities.

"The result would be that one, two, or, at most, a half-dozen universities would have powerhouses, with which the rest of the schools would be unable to compete. Those latter institutions, therefore, would be relieved of a great deal of pressure and could rededicate themselves to higher education, and to developing athletic programs truly amateur, involving a greater percentage of their students.

"The games themselves—even the so-called major sports of baseball, basketball, and football—would remain unchanged and would serve the recreational purpose they were originally intended to serve.

"Either the athletic department is going to have to settle for a smaller, albeit equitable, share of the budgetary pie, or the university itself is going to suffer. Unless we start now to view sports in better perspective—to give athletics a priority no higher than they deserve—that choice might be more difficult than it should be."

Senator Byrd remembered that, at one time, colleges and universities had justified enormous expenditures for athletics by saying that the revenues produced by the teams helped to build classrooms and laboratories. But, he decided, "the years have taught us the fallacy of that argument."

He recalled one college that had lobbied in its state legislature for funds to pay professors—while its athletic department had a surplus of $2,300,000 in a separate bank account.

"The story had a happy ending of sorts," he reported skeptically. "The athletic department loaned the university $400,000— and thus, the teams had a school to represent."

Warren S. Brown sat in the new headquarters building of the National Collegiate Athletic Association in Shawnee Mission, Kansas, and considered the odds: 664 colleges to police and only four investigators to do the policing.

It had been an old story for Brown since he had become the chief policeman for the schools in their ceaseless search for sports talent. Besides the four investigators, Brown was armed with a 4,500-word section of a booklet titled *National Collegiate Athletic Association Bylaws*. The section itself was headed "Recruiting," and in seven segments it covered the "do's and don'ts" of the problem. The chief "don't" was: don't offer a high-school boy or girl more than room, board, tuition, books, and $15 a month for laundry and other incidental expenses.

In spite of the clear language in the booklet, Brown found that some coaches paid as much as $2,000 a year in cash to certain athletes or kept them supplied with season tickets that could be sold for a small fortune.

As a result of Brown's efforts, penalties were imposed on violators at the rate of about twenty per year, and investigations

were pursued against many more. But whenever he tried to get the
member colleges to increase his tiny staff of policemen, he ran into
trouble. Some colleges, like the University of Texas and Notre
Dame, said they would contribute money to a special fund to beef
up the enforcement staff. But nobody else got on the bandwagon
and, at the annual convention of the N.C.A.A., a proposal to add
to Brown's patrol by greater appropriations was voted down.

It was ironic, Brown thought. The same member colleges not
long ago *had* voted to spend a million and one-half dollars to
construct the new headquarters building in Shawnee Mission where
he sat fretting over the whole problem.

In the small city of Oneida, in upstate New York, Francis
Matteo was reading the sports pages with the growing feeling that
he'd been there before. He reached for a file of old letters and
clippings, pulled out a copy of *The New York Times* of Tuesday,
May 24, 1949, and read Arthur Daley's column "Sports of The
Times," which said in part:

> "Some time ago this corner received an indignant letter from
> Francis P. Matteo of Oneida, N.Y. Here's what he says:
> " 'I played football at Syracuse during Chick Meehan's under-
> graduate days there. Then I played professional ball with or against
> such stalwarts as George Halas, Curly Lambeau, Hunk and Eddie
> Anderson, Paddy Driscoll, your own Lou Little (when he was with
> the Yellow Jackets), and so forth. . . . Present-day collegiate foot-
> ball is rotten (morally). Colleges have two ways of proselytizing
> athletes. One is used by the more fashionable and reputable
> schools. This is for an alumnus or group of alumni to "take care
> of" a boy who shows unusual capabilities as a football player.
> Some even have prep schools which serve as "farms" for these
> "major league" colleges.
> " 'This class of college usually has nip-and-tuck battles be-
> tween the alumni and the directors (presidents, etc.). Usually the
> directors are the restraining influence. When they are in the driver's
> seat, the teams are usually fair to mediocre. When the alumni take
> over—wow!—the sky is the limit. What's become of those great
> teams at N.Y.U., Fordham, Pitt, W. & J., etc.? You know.

" 'Now for the second class of colleges that have winning football teams. This class is represented by schools in a certain section of the country. These come right out and practically advertise their rates for football players.

" 'I personally believe that a boy who plays college football should be paid. The sport is of such a nature that pure amateurism would be difficult to maintain throughout the collegiate world. The question naturally arises—how much to pay these athletes? Ah! There's the rub.

" 'No sport presents a sadder picture than two football teams playing against each other—one consisting of "paid" hands and the other consisting of pure or mixed amateurs. A player on the inferior team is more liable to injury, physical as well as mental. What fun is there for a boy to be playing on a losing team that is being overwhelmed? How did the word *fun* get in there? In intercollegiate football, there just ain't no such animal.' "

Mr. Matteo looked back to the sports pages and the old feeling came rushing back. He then reached for a pen and some white stationery and wrote to the *Times* with a clear hand and the same clear conviction:

"Your recent articles on college sports took me back about 25 years to the time I sent Arthur Daley a letter covering the same sordid subject. . . ."

Charles Lewis, a linebacker at Long Beach State in California, turned it all over in his mind and concluded that he was indeed getting a lot of attention. Specifically, he was the center of attention in twenty-three football violations charged by the N.C.A.A. against his university, five of them applying exclusively to Charles Lewis.

One of the charges alleged that he had received credit for some courses at Long Beach State while attending San Francisco City College, 400 miles away. Another charge asserted that, without his knowledge, he was getting credit at the same time from two other colleges. Another stated that his relatives had been guests in free motel rooms when they attended home football games. According to still another, Charley received pocket money from an assistant coach and a "booster," and so on.

The most remarkable achievement of Charley Lewis to come under fire, though, was his academic record: while being marked "present" at four schools on the Pacific Coast at the same time, he presumably earned credit in such courses as "Golf," "Advanced Modern Techniques of Coaching Basketball," and "Officiating Men's Spring Sports." And, as the pièce de résistance: he got straight "A's."

In his own defense, the hotly wooed linebacker remembered that, on his first visit to Long Beach, he had been met at the airport by a delegation of two assistant coaches who opened the relationship by handing him $35 as spending money and who gave him $15 more when they reached the motel.

"I thought, wow, these are outta-sight coaches," Charley Lewis said. "When I got back to San Francisco City College and decided to stay and get my junior-college degree, [the two coaches] flew in from Long Beach and cranked up a deal right there at the airport. If I signed, I wouldn't have to go to school at Long Beach the first semester, just come for spring practice and they would take care of the grades. So I signed. They were buying me and they were buying grades."

Tommy Barker was seven feet tall and sensationally well traveled—even more widely traveled, if possible, than Charley Lewis. Indeed, he was so widely traveled that neither his laundry nor his press clippings could catch up with him.

As a basketball player at Southern Idaho, he was so good that he was promptly named to the junior-college All-America team. He was a sophomore then and that made him happy, especially since he had started college at the University of Minnesota, where he had grown unhappy. So he had transferred to Southern Idaho, fulfilled his promise as a seven-foot basketball player—and then began to grow unhappy again.

So Tommy Barker decided to move again. He signed a letter

of intent with North Carolina State in the Atlantic Coast Conference, transferred from Southern Idaho, stayed at North Carolina State briefly—and found that he was once more growing unhappy.

"The longer I stayed, the more unhappy I became," he recalled. "I was pressured into going there, not so much by the coach but by friends and relatives. They told me to go to North Carolina State and play with David Thompson."

As things turned out, he did go, but he didn't stay long enough to play with David Thompson or anybody else. "I'm the one who is going to be happy or unhappy, not them," he concluded, referring to the "friends and relatives" who had pressured him into making yet another stop on his strange college merry-go-round.

Having been happy three times and unhappy three times at three colleges in two years, Tommy Barker then found a ray of real happiness: the University of Hawaii. He flew there in the summer of 1974, landed at Honolulu, and explained that, even without him, North Carolina State had attained its goal of defeating the University of California at Los Angeles and winning the N.C.A.A. basketball championship.

"The longer I stayed there, the more unhappy I became," he said, repeating the old refrain.

Some people noted that he hadn't stayed at State long enough to become terribly unhappy. But it was *his* frame of mind that was important, not anyone else's. He was attending his *fourth* college in two years and still had two seasons of eligibility in basketball left. His goal, Tommy Barker said, was to be happy as a person, not as a basketball player.

Then, more or less happy, he turned to the future, unpacked his frequently packed bags and added:

"I'd like to help Hawaii achieve its goal of getting to the top."

The Class of 1974 had just graduated, and at Providence College a basketball player named Marvin Barnes got the ultimate graduation present: he was drafted by rival professional teams in rival professional leagues. They were the Philadelphia 76ers of the National Basketball Association and the Denver Rockets of the American Basketball Association. To Barnes, and to other similarly blessed members of the class across the country, that meant one great thing: an auction market with Marvin Barnes on the block, while the bidding went higher and higher.

"They couldn't get me for less than a million," he announced, meaning the Philadelphia team, "or I'd rather work in a factory."

When the coach of the 76ers, Gene Shue, was told of Barnes's estimate, he threw back his head and laughed. "I don't know what they're paying in factories," Shue said. "Guys in factories work hard for their money. I'm sure he has read in the newspapers what players are getting. He has a pretty good personality. I don't think he means it."

But Barnes hadn't gone through four years of college for nothing. He graduated with a firm grasp of such key subjects as economics, psychology, and mathematics—at least to the extent that he could hold his own in the world of pro sports in the 1970s. Unruffled by Coach Shue's badinage, he observed that the Denver Rockets were waiting in the wings with checkbook in hand, and he said with unusual confidence for a young man just leaving college: "I want all I can get."

In Milwaukee, it was the "day after," too—the day after graduation. But Al McGuire, the basketball coach, had something more on his mind than shaking hands and saying good-by to the graduating seniors. McGuire had just learned that he was saying good-by to a "graduating" junior; Maurice Lucas, the star center on his basketball team, had just decided to skip his senior year, accept the draft call of the Chicago Bulls, and graduate directly into pro ball without his degree—and without playing center for McGuire the following season.

The coach was so upset when he got the news that he refused to talk about it. But he finally unburdened his soul the next day.

Lucas, he reflected, had been snatched out of college because of a provision in the pro rules that allows a club to draft an undergraduate in certain "hardship" circumstances—if staying in school would work a hardship on the boy. But McGuire suspected, as many coaches did, that the real hardship would be on the pro team if the boy stayed in college.

"Everybody knocks the hooker on the corner and the junkie in the hallway," McGuire said. "But some of our most reputable people work more in the shadows than in the sunlight. They are not allowing young people to live at the age they are at."

Coach McGuire, it seemed, had not formed that opinion on the spur of the moment. The year before, the best junior on the Marquette team, Larry McNeill, had turned pro. And the year before that, the top junior, on the Marquette team, Jim Chones, had done the same thing. It was getting to be a "hardship" every blooming year.

At Athens, Ohio, a man named Meade Burnett announced that he was leaving college, too—at the age of forty-two. He was the track and cross-country coach at Ohio University, and he was giving it all up *not* to turn pro. Meade Burnett was finding the college sports system too much of a strain on his conscience.

"For the past two years," he said, "I have been studying the Bible very hard and now am one of the Jehovah's Witnesses. I feel there are certain compromises that present-day coaches must make in accepting the morality of today, and I can no longer accept these.

"I think the question I have asked myself—and this is not a reflection on only Ohio University—has to do with the standard which has been accepted on all of our major campuses. It's basically because of the permissive attitude of the universities, simply because it is more important for them to fill an enrollment quota than it is to hold the lines on necessary disciplines of our young people.

"Many major universities find it difficult to say no to student pressure for fear of losing dollars. Instead of building up our young people, we let them come to the universities and let them become less than what they were morally when they started.

"As a person in a position of recruiting young men to leave their homes and move to a university—and possibly live in some dormitory situations where there is a lack of discipline, exposing them to the availability of drugs without a certain amount of parental guidance—[I reached the point] where I could no longer do these things."

"Again," he said, "I don't mean only Ohio University. I'm not taking any cheap shots at anybody."

The athletic director, Burnett's immediate superior, said he was "extremely sorry" to lose the coach and added, "We naturally must accede to the man's personal religious convictions and wish him well in his new life."

So Meade Burnett turned his back on the campus scene, gathered his wife and four children, and prepared to move to Greensburg, Indiana. He planned to join a small congregation there and spend his life raising cattle.

CHAPTER II

The Slave
Market

America's campuses, which were rocked by student unrest in the sixties, are being shaken by a new crisis in the seventies: a frenzied "slave market" in the recruiting and paying of athletes.

The term is probably not used by the athletes who are recruited and paid, nor by the athletic directors and coaches who send their scouts combing the country for talent, nor by the presidents of the universities that need the clamor and cash of big-time sports to maintain images or pay bills. But many educators, well-shuffled athletes and even battle-weary coaches have begun to realize that we are faced with a public scandal. And they have attributed this to a national mania to "win at any cost." A mania that is thriving in other levels of public life, from the exploration of space to the grim gamesmanship of geopolitics. But to "win *at any cost*" on a basketball court?

The *cost* is spreading far beyond the 50,000 athletes and coaches who stage 32,000 basketball and 3,000 football games during a college year, and beyond the hundreds of millions of dollars which the games are generating. The *cost*, the skeptics charge, is being paid in the growing corruption of high-school students, in the distortion of the role of sports in education, and in the moral climate surrounding the schools and colleges.

Even a successful coach like Frank Broyles of the University of Arkansas has predicted that "if something isn't done, the lid is going to blow off." And, forty-five years after a historic study of identical pressures, the Carnegie Corporation, the Ford Foundation, and other national bodies have initiated inquiries into the gold-rush world of college sports.

It has been the best of times; it has been the worst of times. Each spring, thousands of high-school seniors sweat out their admission to college, while an elite group of quarterbacks and 6-foot-8-inch centers ponder over which high-powered offers to accept before the deadline known as "national signing day." Certain conferences schedule their own deadlines—Bear Bryant's Air Force will have long since completed its missions across the Southeast. But the witching hour for most football heroes in the Class of 1974 came one morning early in March, and for all other athletes one day in mid-April.

Nobody denies that this grab-bag frenzy will open college doors to some students, especially black and women athletes, who might otherwise have stayed home. But to many observers, the system more often ends in the exploitation of the young persons whom it supposedly is glorifying—even though colleges like Ohio State spend $4,000,000 a year on sports and U.C.L.A. budgets $500,000 for athletic scholarships.

"It's the worst I've seen in my twenty-three years of coaching," said Joe Paterno, whose football team earned $500,000 for Penn State in the 1974 Orange Bowl game.

"It's not the kids, it's the system," said Digger Phelps, the basketball coach at Notre Dame, whose football team earned $420,000 in the 1974 Sugar Bowl and whose basketball team made history by ending U.C.L.A.'s eighty-eight-game winning streak in 1974.

"Football is just too big," said Tim O'Shea when he was a senior majoring in engineering at the University of Nebraska.

"You know something has gone amiss when the stadium [which seats 76,000 persons] is the third largest city in the state on a home-game day."

"It's getting vicious again," said the Rev. Ed Visscher, basketball coach at Long Island Lutheran High School, perennially one of the best teams in the country. "The competition reminds me of the old slave markets, talking about 'things' instead of 'people.' Budgets are getting tighter, pressure is coming down from above, the schools are reaching the point of 'win or else.' "

More and more symptoms of runaway professionalism can be seen at all levels of education. The following are examples:

Nine of every ten college athletic departments are running in the red. The chief reason is that costs have doubled in the last decade, and in some cases in the last five years. The chief result has been a steepening of the competition for high-school athletes who might thrust a college into the national limelight, the television picture, the postseason bowl games—or just into the black.

Forty-one colleges have dropped football in the last ten years —eight of them in one year alone—because the pressure has become so great. Don Canham, athletic director at the University of Michigan, warned that, if the trend continued, only the biggest would survive and "a super conference will develop out of the wreckage."

In their rush for teen-age talent, universities are increasingly ignoring or sidestepping the nine pages of single-spaced rules that form the heart of the recruiting code of the N.C.A.A. In the booklet on Warren Brown's desk in Shawnee Mission, Kansas, the key provision still says that a college may provide only tuition, room, board, books, and $15 a month for "laundry."

But some violations include payments to high-school stars, tampering with their grades, forging their transcripts, finding substitutes to take their exams, promising jobs to their parents, buying them cars, and supplying them with football tickets that can be scalped for as much as $8,000 during their undergraduate careers.

At U.C.L.A., several eager alumni once secretly posted a bounty of $5 for every rebound off the basketball backboard.

The 664 colleges in the N.C.A.A. are still being policed by the four investigators led by Brown, who once did all of the investigating himself, plus six others who were added in January, 1975. Their job has not been made any easier by the fact that some colleges tend to be "repeaters." Oklahoma was placed on probation three times in seventeen years in football; Southwestern Louisiana, twice in six years during a sudden rise to prominence in basketball; and Cornell, already on probation in hockey, later admitted violations in basketball.

What it all adds up to, many educators agree, is a frantic hustling of the 300,000 football and 200,000 basketball seniors in the nation's 22,000 high schools—or, at least, of the few hundred of them who excel in these money sports.

Some get "letters of interest" from colleges while they are still in the ninth grade. Rick Mount, who went from Purdue University to the American Basketball Association as a high-priced rookie, started getting letters in the eighth grade. Eric Penick of Notre Dame, when he was a star halfback at Gilmour Academy in Cleveland, was besieged by sixty-two college coaches the week after his last game.

The rush is reaching into sports that do not customarily fill stadiums, like swimming, lacrosse, and wrestling, and even into sideshows that do not qualify as sports, like rodeo and baton-twirling. And women athletes have taken their cues. As women have begun to prosper in professional tennis, golf, and horse racing, the co-eds are calling for their share of the campus loot. At the University of Miami, fifteen scholarships were offered in golf, tennis, and swimming—and 400 girls applied from as far away as Hawaii.

Is it all just a cat-and-mouse game between a paid recruiter and an unsuspecting boy, or even between a paid recruiter and a possibly greedy boy? Not to the people caught up in the system. To them, it goes far beyond the heady "pursuit." Coach and athlete may represent the chase itself, but always in the background, supplying external pressure, are the college presidents trying to build stadiums or libraries, the alumni trying to build the prestige of their alma mater, and the state officials trying to build a record for the public that paid the taxes.

But it remains an open question whether their combined efforts result in more opportunities for education or just more opportunities for money. Nobody is knocking money if it happens to be the main result of the system; but the crisis is growing because money seems to be turning into the main goal of the system. And worse, more high-school athletes are winding up with neither a college education nor the money from an elusive career in the pros.

But, whether the high-school player goes the full route or not, many persons complain that the formula still is too "simple," the incentive too commercial—even if there is nothing illegal in taking the boy out of the country and converting him into a millionaire. Horatio Alger and all that, but in this American success story the motivation is becoming outrageously expressed in dollar signs.

Norman Blass, a lawyer who represented such basketball stars as Dave Cowens, Bob Lanier, and Dick Barnett, told in clinical terms "how a youth of 7-foot-4 made a million at twenty-two." He got right to the point:

"Tom Burleson, twenty-two years old, from the hill country of North Carolina, became a millionaire because he was 7 feet 4 inches and lucky enough to be drafted by the Seattle SuperSonics of the National Basketball Association, a team in need of a big man.

"The center is still the big man in pro basketball. Without him, a team can't win consistently. Seattle needed a center to cope with the big men in the Western Conference—Kareem Abdul-Jabbar of the Milwaukee Bucks, Bob Lanier of the Detroit Pistons, Nate Thurmond of the Golden State Warriors, Elmore Smith of the Los Angeles Lakers, and Bill Walton of the Portland Trail Blazers.

"Salaries are not dwindling where the needs of a team are great. The players selected at the top of the college draft list—the Bill Waltons, Tom Burlesons, Marvin Barneses, and the Len Elmores—will get their big money. The lesser players will find it more difficult getting the big bonuses and the no-cut contracts because the American Basketball Association is competing only for the very big name players."

The element of interleague competition, Blass notes, is critical—as is the element of need for height on the basketball floor. Teams like the Boston Celtics and the Milwaukee Bucks already had imposing centers, so Burleson's financial future rested partly on the luck of the draw and partly on the altitude situation of the drawing teams. If he had been drafted by either Milwaukee or Boston, for instance, he would have been offered about half the money he eventually got, despite his talent.

The "outside" pressure was obligingly supplied by the Indiana Pacers of the Rival A.B.A., a league that appeared to be coming apart at some of its outer seams. But the strong teams in the league pressed ahead, dangling fortunes before name players like Tom Burleson in a frantic effort to stay alive on the pro scene.

Accordingly, Burleson when he had finished playing for North Carolina State found himself in an extraordinary sales position when the Carolina Cougars of the A.B.A. won draft rights to him and then assigned the rights to Indiana. All this happened before the N.B.A. had even conducted its own draft. So when the Indiana club intensified its bid to sign him, Norman Blass and his partner, Len Snyder, decided that time was on their side. They insisted on waiting for the N.B.A. draft so that "all counties would be heard from."

"Prior to the draft," Blass reported in his account of the transaction, "we were almost certain that the Phoenix Suns would take Burleson. They had been in touch with us continually the previous two weeks. But when Seattle traded Dick Snyder to the Cleveland Cavaliers at the last moment for the rights to pick ahead of the Suns, the situation changed.

"After the draft, Bill Russell, the Sonic general manager, called us to talk about Burleson. We spoke about him on the telephone three or four times, and when progress was made we invited Sam Shulman, the Seattle owner, and Dick Tinkham, the vice-president of the Indiana Pacers, to come to New York to present and finalize their offers.

"It was not our intention to have them bid against each other, but to have them realize that it was close to decision-making time and to put forth their best offers. We gave them a certain perimeter, but did not allow any bartering."

That is, no bartering around the auction block. But both teams appreciated the situation: Tom Burleson was in the driver's seat, with the advice and consent of his father and the family attorney. It was not exactly the same situation that faced the average college graduate in search of a first job.

"We presented both packages," Blass recalled, "and he evaluated the money offered by each, the basis of payment, the length of each contract proposal, the prestige and stability of the respective leagues, the distance from home, the coach for whom he would play, and other related factors.

"Both offers were no-cut, guaranteed contracts, so this was not a consideration. However, with all these factors, it was important to note that the Seattle monetary offer was better, and with the N.B.A. stability, this alone would have been sufficient to convince Tom to accept the Seattle offer."

Burleson's situation was somewhat different from that of the average senior, actually, because he was still a few points short of his degree. For a major in chemistry, no sale; for a basketball center, no problem. The contract called for big money, an "incentive bonus" if he became the N.B.A. rookie of the year, and payment of any college costs if he decided to return to college within two years to polish off his degree. On-the-job training, so to speak.

"Nothing else," Blass noted with satisfaction. "Some other contracts have included such things as annuities, cars, apartments, and jobs for families in lieu of cash, but Tom didn't want any of those.

"Seattle has paid Tom a bundle of money. I remember Russell's words at the signing: 'The agreement is between Wells Fargo and Jesse James.' "

Blass said his fee for representing Jesse James was 5 percent, and nobody could argue with that. Nobody, in fact, could argue with any of it, not even Wells Fargo. The only rub is that the colleges themselves are being drawn by the magnet of money into bidding for athletes half-a-dozen years younger than Tom Burleson, and at that level of operation—from high school to college, even before the long arm of the pros begins to reach into the talent pool—more and more boys are turning into copies of Jesse James. There is indeed gold in the hills, and the stampede is on.

The situation has been getting so acute that even the coaches decided to take a look. The National Association of Basketball Coaches took a poll of twenty-five athletics directors, twenty-five former college players who had been All-America selections in high school, twenty-five high-school players who had All-America ranking at the time, and the parents of twenty-five such stars. In a way, they were heading off Jesse James at the pass.

The poll was voted during a wave of protests from the coaching benches, where the situation was getting very sticky. Pete Newell, a longtime college basketball coach who became general manager of the Los Angeles Lakers, put it this way, "The prevailing thought is that 'if he can do it, why can't I?' " And Bob Cousy, the onetime Boston Celtics whiz, weary and frustrated by the day-to-day struggle, quit after a long career in basketball coaching and said, "It wasn't worth it, the winning and losing and everything else."

When Jack Rohan resigned as Columbia's basketball coach in 1973, he fired this parting shot: "I leave with a great deal of sadness. Also, with a warning that you get the N.C.A.A. to come down hard on recruiting cheaters. Otherwise, we'll have a major scandal again."

Another inquiry has been started by the American Council on Education with financial help from the Ford Foundation and the Carnegie Corporation, and with some prompting from the Association of American Universities. In Ottawa, meanwhile, a major study of sports has been undertaken by the Association of Universities and Colleges of Canada.

The studies were the first of such scope since 1929, when the Carnegie Foundation for the Advancement of Education issued a historic report on the fact that "college sports have been developed from games played by boys for pleasure into systematic professionalized athletic contests."* But it is now clear that any sweeping new investigation into the marketplace of college sports will have to cover a lot of ground to keep up with the situation as it exists today.

When Louisiana State's football team went to the Orange Bowl in Miami for the 1974 game, the fuel shortage that was besetting the nation had made serious inroads into the school's extracurricular life. The university was forced to cancel the charter flight for the marching band. But all was not lost. Commercial space *was* booked on an airliner—at a cost of $25,000.

When Frank Navarro quit as Columbia's football coach in November, 1973, he was succeeded by Bill Campbell, who said (in a voice made hoarse by the constant recruiting speeches that he had been making for Boston College), "My main goal is to intensify recruiting efforts by alumni in all parts of the country. The alumni have to take an active part in luring kids to come to Columbia."

When the University of Oklahoma finished its football season in 1973 under probation, an imaginative plan was suggested by the athletic director, Wade Walker: sell season tickets between the forty-yard lines to the highest bidders, with an opening price of $1,000. "When you compete with the Joneses," he said, not betraying any signs of the probation blues, "you'd better have a program like the Joneses."

When Notre Dame ended U.C.L.A.'s winning basketball streak at eighty-eight games in January, 1974, the great event was

* Excerpts from the 1929 report appear in Chapter XII and in Appendix I.

watched by a sellout crowd at South Bend, a national television audience, and twenty-eight special guests: high-school football stars who were spending the weekend at Notre Dame, all expenses paid. If they needed any further prompting in the educational decision which all of them faced, they probably got it from the spectacle taking place on the basketball court. They were in the right place at the right time.

When Leonard Thompson, a twenty-seven-year-old golfer, won his first tournament as a professional in 1974—the Jackie Gleason Inverrary at Fort Lauderdale, Florida—he pocketed the purse of $52,000 and recalled his student days at Wake Forest. What did he study in college? "Golf," Thompson replied, absolutely in tune with the times. "If you don't believe me, ask my professors."

But for total involvement, probably nothing reflects the trend more than the city of Petersburg, Virginia, where a 6-foot-11-inch high-school senior not long ago set a record for leading the country in promises received. His name is Moses Malone, and he was averaging 38 points and 26 rebounds a game in the 1973–74 season, while his basketball team was winning games by 50 points before standing-room-only crowds. The promises for such élan included tuition, room, board, books, $15 a month for "laundry" —and a car, an apartment, and cash.

The post office even sent out a Christmas message inscribed, in the spirit of the season—the basketball season, that is—"Greetings from Petersburg, home of Moses Malone."

To Moses, though, it was all a little heady, even though one basketball super-scout described his potential as a member of the Class of 1974 in these words:

"He can lead any college program in the nation into the promised land."

If that scouting report seemed a little exuberant to some persons, it apparently did not trouble the nation's colleges. More than 300 of them, about one-fourth of all those that field basketball teams in the United States, offered him scholarships—even though he had posted only a "C" average in high school.

He was still a teen-age phenomenon surrounded by uncommon attention, the tallest boy or man in sight, the poor kid known as "Jughead" in the neighborhood because of the prominent head on top of the tall body, the self-conscious student who would mumble some excuse and sit down quickly if he was asked to recite in class.

While Moses pondered which of the 300 college offers to accept, his high-school athletic career ended on the upbeat along his high-school academic career: he managed a "B" average in his final semester. This led to some whispers that Petersburg High was making a genius of a mediocre student in order to get him into college.

"To hear some of the stories," said Bob Kilbourne, the school's athletic director, "you'd think we were making him a scholar in chemistry or some such subject. But a lot of people don't know that Moses was a 'C' student all the time here. In his last term he got a 'B' average, but he took mostly easy subjects. There was nothing unusual about that."

Kilbourne explained that Moses had received a "C" in English, "and his English teacher spent a lot of time helping him get that—he got a lot of special tutoring." He also took woodworking, and got a "B." Also art, for a "B." And speech, for an "A."

"To appreciate that mark," the athletic director said, "you've got to understand what Moses was when he came in. He came a long way here. You don't grade his speech the way you'd grade President Ford. You grade him on how he improved and how he now could speak before his class."

When all the offers, whispers, shouts, and hurrahs had subsided, Moses finally made his choice of which college basketball program he would "lead into the promised land." The winner: the University of Maryland.

But during the summer, between the time he graduated from Petersburg High and the time he was expected to reach the Mary-

(*The New York Times/William E. Sauro*)
With his mother at his side, Moses Malone of Petersburg High School in Virginia—19 years old and 6-foot-11—makes history with one stroke of the pen: straight into professional basketball with the Utah Stars for a million-dollar contract.

land campus, the "system" catapulted Moses Malone from the sports pages into the history pages. He was still only nineteen years old, he still had never played basketball beyond high school, and he still had not even started the college career that figured to add substantially to his stature—and to his eventual price. But, in spite of his youth and inexperience, the pros came running anyway. And before the summer was out, Moses had received the full pitch: turn pro now, go to college later, and wind up with the best of both possible worlds.

He did. Skipping the scholarship that he had won at Maryland, he signed with the Utah Stars of the American Basketball Association and became the first player in basketball history to vault directly from high school into the pros. He went first-class, too: he landed a seven-year deal with a potential value of $3 million, including such options as a bonus of $30,000 for every year of college that he might complete if he decided to attend in the off-season.

So Moses Malone passed up the chance to "lead any college program in the nation into the promised land." But he took his high-school diploma and his $3 million and headed—a remarkable symbol of the sports gold rush—into a promised land of his own.

CHAPTER III

The Hunter
and the Hunted

Tournament time in New York City. The top schools are heading for the championship rounds, and motels on the outskirts of town are suddenly getting calls from Chapel Hill, North Carolina, and Columbia, South Carolina, and Omaha, Nebraska, and El Paso, Texas, and Long Beach, California. Scouts and recruiters want rooms.

There remains a magic about the New York high-school basketball player. When Frank McGuire left the city and built a basketball empire at the University of South Carolina, he started something dubbed the "Underground Railroad." He pirated the best from New York. Why?

"There's something about a New York kid," he reasoned. "Maybe it's because he's grown up and had to learn to dodge subway trains. No one else in the country ever had to do that. The New York kid learns to think on his feet faster than anyone else."

Since a lot of people around the country have at least one relative, or friend, or friend of a friend in New York, it has become natural for college coaches to get word on the latest schoolboy hero—and, just as quickly, to draw a bead on him. After a fast check on his classroom grades—if the college in question

(*The New York Times/Larry Morris*)

Most likely to succeed, Class of 1974: Alfred (Butch) Lee, star guard on the DeWitt Clinton High School basketball team in New York City, rarely lacks reading material—300 letters from 200 colleges, all wanting him to come play ball.

cares about grades—the next decision for the coach to make is: Do we need this boy? What kind of chance do we have to land him?

If the answer to the first question is yes, the coach sends out his recruiter, usually the assistant basketball coach, and leaves the answer to the second question up to him.

The techniques vary, just as techniques vary among vacuum-cleaner salesmen or Fuller Brush men. The colleges that are confident of their "product"—basketball, in this case—don't have to try as hard as the up-and-coming little colleges that are on the make to grab reputations.

Here is the story of a young man who heard from many of them: one-fifth of all the colleges that field a basketball team in the United States wrote to him. And there is also a parallel story, of the school that wooed him and won him, and how it did it.

Nighttime in Harlem. The insistent lights from the pizza parlor and candy store and liquor shop filtered through the vestibule into the rundown building at Eighth Avenue and 153rd Street. Butch Lee was just coming home from another practice.

He was a senior now, and basketball practice took up most of his free time. He opened the mailbox, fished out the "three more" letters, and shook his head, almost bored with the ritual. He walked up the five flights ("Good for the legs," he rationalized), turned the key in the lock, then a second key, and he was inside his apartment.

"This is my room," he said. He turned on the light and looked around. The paint on the walls was a memory, and the plaster on the ceiling hung like stalactites. It filled the room with long shadows whenever the dangling light bulb swayed. The dreams were under his bed.

"Here they are," he said. Tenderly—one was surprised to find tenderness in this setting—he pulled out the three shoe boxes stuffed with 300 letters. And there they were: the bait offered in a continuing chase for the young black basketball star who lived in this bare little apartment uptown.

He had long since realized the pattern of the chase, the stakes, the deadlines. He was the mouse and somebody else was the cat. He was the target and somebody else was the sharpshooter. There was a hunter—and he was the hunted.

More than 200 colleges wrote to Alfred (Butch) Lee to tell him they wanted him to play basketball for them. He was the most heavily recruited guard in the United States.

But Butch was laconic, and if he appreciated the noise made over him, he never showed it. He didn't even appear disturbed when more than twenty recruiters visited him at DeWitt Clinton High School in the Bronx. Perhaps his coach, young and bearded John Wyles, helped shepherd Lee along.

"I'm on this damn phone half the day answering questions about Butch," Wyles complained. But he was generally good-natured about it. He would allow recruiters to come to the school when it was convenient for him and Butch. He knew what it could mean for Butch, but he also knew that he wanted his star to keep a level head.

Butch was seventeen years old, six feet tall, and very muscular. His grades were above average, for Clinton, at 82. That placed him 161st in a class of about a thousand. But his S.A.T.'s averaged 450, not scores that would make a guidance counselor sanguine about the average student. Butch wasn't average.

He received so many recruiting letters from Marquette that his name was on an Addressograph. He got more than twenty letters from Detroit, each written by the coach with a felt-tip marker. Coach Lefty Driesell of Maryland, who never met him and didn't even know where he lived, sent him a telegram at school wishing him luck in the Public Schools Athletic League tournament. Butch had a lot of sudden friends.

He ran his fingers over the letters: Penn, West Virginia, Washington State, Dayton, Duquesne. They came from all over, north and south, east and west. Warm climates, cold climates. Colleges that promised four years away from Eighth Avenue. At first, the letters had filled only one Converse "All-Star" shoe box.

Then they came in torrents, and accompanied by expensively printed four-color brochures.

"I don't mind it," he said. "But it's kind of crazy when you get so many offers, you know. I can't always talk to the coaches when I'm in school, so I tell a lot of them to call me after eleven at night after I come home from my girl friend's."

The coaches called whenever Butch said they should. They courted him at midnight, after he had finished his own courting.

When Butch Lee was seven, he came from St. Thomas, in the Virgin Islands, with his parents, an older brother, and a younger sister. His father managed a bar and his mother was a legal secretary. In Butch's senior year, his father returned to the Virgin Islands to build a house. The plan was for the rest of the family to move back to the Islands after Butch started college.

Soon after arriving in Harlem, Butch picked up a basketball. He doesn't know why—"but I guess I was always better than the other kids my age." In the summertime, he swept the cement court of the playground across the street where the celebrated Rucker tournament was staged. "No one never really taught me," Butch remembered.

"Where people really started to hear about me was after I went to this summer camp right after my junior year. I met this man named Garfinkel, and he told me that if I went to his place everyone would know who I was. But I wasn't interested in going. I changed my mind."

The "man named Garfinkel" was Howard Garfinkel, a New Yorker who runs an extraordinary marketplace—at a summer camp in Pennsylvania. Instead of displaying carcasses, he shows another sort of beef: prime. He showcases the hot shooters in high-school basketball. Each summer, more than 100 college coaches show up at Garfinkel's camp—and every boy there knows it. And when the summer ends, Garfinkel prepares a "tout" sheet listing the assets and liabilities of each boy. He charges $150 for his information, and sells it to more than 100 colleges.

If you want to make sure your name is on that sheet, you attend his camp—for a fee, of course.

"He only charged me $60 a week," Butch said. "I got a cut rate because I waited on tables."

In a well-scouted game at camp, Lee set a single-game record with fifty points. The mailbox in Harlem was filled when he got back. The phone started to ring. The recruiters began visiting the school.

Now Butch is sitting in a teacher's lounge at Clinton High. The room is public-school drab—dull green paint, scratched desks. A coffee urn. High windows. He is flanked by two men from Marquette University in Milwaukee. He is fixed between their stares, as if each had a gunsight and had found the range.

"What's the weather like down there?" Butch asks.

"Oh . . ." The response is guarded. "The summer's hot and the winter's cold."

"But, Butch, it's a dry cold," says the other recruiter.

Then Lee wants to know whether Coach Al McGuire will remain at Marquette or take a job in the pros. The pros, Butch Lee knows, are on the mind of every right-thinking person in basketball. What if Butch went to Marquette in order to learn under the cool hand of Al McGuire, only to discover that McGuire has deserted him? Butch has learned how to ask the right questions.

"Coach just signed a five-year contract with us, Butch," explains one recruiter. "He's not going to break it. You know you'll have him for your four years."

"I've got to pull him away now," interrupts Coach Wyles. "It's practice time."

For the next two and one-half hours, Lee worked out in the school gym, under high windows painted black to keep the sunlight out of the players' eyes. He was in a class by himself as he moved effortlessly and expertly through the passing drills, the man-to-man defense coverage, the shooting. While he practiced, the recruiters eyed him. Perspiration—beads of excitement—formed over their lips, and they followed every move.

Later, he explained that he hadn't been nervous—"I play the same whether someone's watching me or not. I'm used to having people look at me."

His mother wanted him to go to an Ivy League college. She preferred Penn, which was interested in him. Penn, in fact, was so interested that Princeton investigated to learn whether Penn had behaved legally. In the Ivies, you don't get in touch with a prospect until his season is over. Butch liked the idea of Penn and was flattered. But he also liked the idea of Duke, Detroit, or Marquette even more. Still, he wasn't sure.

"In my position," he said, "a lot of people want me to do this, do that. I'm getting so much advice. Utah told me I'll get a lot of pro exposure. But my mother wants to know if I'll get tutoring if I need it."

As a senior, he had plenty of time to look over the offers. Most of his "major" subjects needed for graduation had already been taken.

It was toward the end of the term. It was already spring. Lee showed displeasure for the first time as late offers came in. "When they come in now," he explained, "I feel like I'm only second-best, like they've already looked at some other guys and now they're coming after me."

He was slowly becoming as cool in the real world as he had been on the court for most of his life. The initial warm glow of being wanted had started to cool, and now there were calculated decisions to be made. Ultimately, he could decide what was best for him. He had a choice, something that most of the students in the United States, even those with grades far better than his, did not have.

"I guess the two things I'm looking for is the academic and the basketball," he said. "I want the degree. But where? Like I won't go to Maryland. I saw that John Lucas play on television— and he don't give up the ball. I'm a guard. I have to figure that I'm going to have the ball."

The reaction of Butch's mother to all this amused him.

. . . only six feet tall and 17 years old, but everybody wanted to recruit Butch Lee and many scouts made the journey to the Bronx gymnasium to watch No. 35 scrimmage.

"When the recruiters come to the house, she asks them if I'll even get to play. She doesn't know how good I am."

He tamped the letters down in the shoe boxes and put them back under his bed. He locked the door and walked down the stairs. When he got to the third floor, a neighbor spotted him. The man was weaving and holding the stair railing for support.

"Hey, Butch," he called, "you make up your mind yet about school?"

And as Butch walked down, the man shouted after him again: "Butch, you go to college, you hear? You go away to school and get your degree. God bless you, Butch."

Six weeks later, Butch Lee accepted one of the offers that had cascaded into the apartment on Eighth Avenue—Marquette. He entered the school in the fall of 1974, and the chase was over.

A grateful and happy coach, Al McGuire, sent out locker-room passes to everyone who had played a part in getting Butch Lee to attend Marquette. The passes are good only after games that the team wins.

It had been the usual long day for Rick Majerus, the twenty-five-year-old recruiter for Marquette University's basketball team. But it was the sort of day that he loved, indeed lived for. Sometimes it appeared that he would explode with happiness. His good fortune was being able to take a look at some of the best young basketball players in the United States.

The day had begun while Butch Lee was still asleep in Harlem. Majerus took an early-morning drive to West New York, a New Jersey suburb, to take a look at a promising ballplayer. Then he waited on line for ninety minutes to get gasoline. And finally, he made a trek that was a sort of pilgrimage, a trek to the Bronx to talk to Lee of DeWitt Clinton. Lee was the most heavily recruited guard in the United States, and Majerus, a portly young man given to sweating easily, would have to be cool this day. He had help— Jack Burke, a twenty-seven-year-old, clean-cut, All-America sort who had been the captain of Marquette's National Invitation

Tournament champions of 1970. Burke was in the mortgage-insurance business in New Jersey, but he gladly offered his time to Marquette to try to convince blue-chip athletes that Marquette was the place to be.

The Majerus-Burke team was not unlike a pair of homicide detectives grilling a suspect. Majerus would be the heavy, planting the ideas into the "suspect's" head. Burke would be the "nice guy," keeping things on an even keel in case the suspect worried too much about Majerus's tough approach.

Majerus's formal title at the college was "assistant coach," a title that a coach at another major power dismissed as "crap." He explained: "All assistant coaches are recruiters. That's all."

Majerus had flown in from Milwaukee at the college's expense. But, as with most of his incidental expenses, he paid the tolls out of his own pocket. It was almost as if he were so happy doing this job that he felt guilty getting paid for it.

"We've only got a $5,000-a-year recruiting budget," he said. "For other schools, that's tipping money."

To save on housing and food, he had spent the night at Burke's home. After the trip to West New York, the two set off for the Bronx ("How the heck can you find the place?" Majerus asked).

They found the place. By previous arrangement with Butch's coach, John Wyles, they were permitted to speak to Lee at the school. Majerus sat at Lee's left, within whispering distance. Burke sat at the boy's right. There was a body language of sorts at work. They had enclosed Lee, forming a tight little island that made for instant camaraderie. The whispering heightened the effect, as if there were secrets to be shared by just the three of them.

"Irregardless of race or creed, you'll get your chance," Majerus told Butch.

"You're not going to believe this, Butch," said Burke, "but Milwaukee is like a small New York."

Lee asked only a few questions in the twenty minutes, and

most of them were of the devil's advocate sort. For a brief moment, it appeared, Burke got a bit annoyed.

"You know, Butch, we're not going to come back here every other day and hold your hand," said Burke. "We know what we've got to offer. We don't have to go around begging people."

Majerus, stressing the advantages of playing on the Marquette team under Coach Al McGuire, said, "The media knows Al. Al tries to get his boys exposure for the pros. Why, Red Holzman wants him as an assistant coach for the Knicks. Everyone knows Al McGuire."

"We're on national television," added Burke.

"You're our Number One boy now," said Majerus. "Believe me, Butch, we won't bring in any guards behind you or ahead of you. You'll get your chance to show what you can do."

Then Majerus remembered something that he had often heard from boys who visited his campus after having seen some other high-powered colleges with sprawling campuses and deluxe locker rooms.

"You know, Butch, a lot of kids complained about our locker room. They'd visit some big power school, and there'd be red carpeting and beautiful lockers. But, Butch, after four years, what good does the carpeting do you?"

Wyles interrupted the conversation. "Butch has to go to practice now," he said.

Majerus finally was ready to ask the question, and he tried to be cool about it. Rejection is always in the back of his mind. "Hey, Butch," he called out as Lee walked toward the gym, "would you like to visit us?"

"Okay," said Lee.

Majerus turned to Burke and sighed.

Upstairs, in the Clinton gym, Majerus watched Lee for only two minutes and said, "Al McGuire would go crazy if he were here. Look at that kid."

Anyone else looking "at that kid" would have seen a baby-faced ballplayer softly popping in jump shots. Really no different from a thousand other black youngsters in schoolyards and gyms all over New York City. He was a bit smoother, perhaps, was coordinated, and did not give the appearance of having his arms and legs strung together and flopping wildly when he went up for a rebound. Majerus, though, had already learned a lot about Butch Lee. He saw in Lee, as he saw in dozens of other youngsters that he had looked at during the last few years, that touch of greatness that had always been lacking in himself.

"My idea of a good time is to go to the coach's room at night and look over the films," he said. "When I was a sophomore at Marquette, Coach McGuire came over to me and said I was the crappiest player he ever saw. He told me to get out of playing, that I had no future. So I became a coach."

But a broad smile came over Majerus's face. He was eyeing Lee, taking in the muscles of the youngster's broad back. Indeed, Majerus might have had the same look if he had been a horse breeder with a mare and was staring at Secretariat. In only a few minutes, Majerus had learned quite a bit about Butch Lee.

"Look at the rotation on the ball on his jump shot," Majerus began. "It spins backwards evenly. See his shots—even when they're long they're in the right direction, not to the side. And when he goes up, the back of his hand is parallel to the floor. There's a wrinkle in his wrist. His elbow is under the ball. You can't teach a kid that."

And just how good was Lee? "Well, our reports said he was the best guard in the city. That usually means the best in the country."

But Marquette also plays a tight defensive game, a hustling New York game that McGuire, who spent his youth on city playgrounds, had learned the hard way. Many black youngsters, some coaches believe, don't want to bother with this aspect of the game. They just want to shoot the damn ball all the time.

One move on defense was all that Majerus needed to be convinced that the boy could fit into Marquette's disciplined defensive style. "Split vision," Majerus said. "You know, a lot of these

The hunters and the hunted: Jack Burke and Rick Majerus tell Butch Lee all about the advantages of a Marquette education, and the young guard listens—and agrees.

inner-city kids don't have the good jump shots like the boys in the suburbs. The kids in the city are always going one-on-one, working the ball in with tricky moves. But in the suburbs, they don't go for the contact inside, so they develop those great jump shots. This kid here—he's an inner-city kid with a suburban jump shot."

Higher praise could a recruiter lavish on no one. Majerus had seen a hand-picked corps of superstars during his days on the trail, but he was somewhat limited by the fact that he didn't go "west of the Mississippi or down South." "The climate and the life-style there is too different," he said. "Not many boys from those places will want to go to Milwaukee."

As a result, Marquette's recruiting wasn't as broadly based as that of most nationally ranked colleges.

"We only talk to ten or twelve kids a year," Majerus said. "So the kids we go after, we really have to make sure we've got a shot at them. We can't afford to run all over the country and make these offers of cars and money that some schools do."

Now he was selling a proven product, but when he started his career as a hunter, recruiting was a chore. When McGuire first tapped him to go on the road, he recalled, "I didn't have confidence and I used to think, 'What if none of the kids I recruited came to the school?' But Coach McGuire was super. He told me the sun will still shine the next day."

In recruiting, it seems, everyone is doing something wrong—except the college you happen to be talking to. Coaches speak of keeping within the rules, of the immorality of chasing youngsters, or of offering something the N.C.A.A. would not approve of. There are recruiting abuses all over the land—"but it's not happening here."

Majerus also defended his college's policies: "Coach McGuire tells his people not to make wild promises. We offer the kid four years at a good school with national exposure and a degree. That's all."

In the summertime, Majerus usually continues his search for the "perfect player" who is also willing to go to Marquette. Although McGuire tells him to "just relax" when school is out, Majerus packs his bag again and sets off in his car to scout the country alone, and at his own expense.

"Sometimes I think I'm the luckiest guy in the world," he said. "I see the best basketball players in the country. I couldn't ask for anything more."

His recruiting style apparently has improved over the years. He has a high rate of return. He spoke proudly of the fact that three boys had visited the Marquette campus the previous year, and two had selected the college. Marquette did fail to get one player who was Jewish, even though Majerus explained to him, "Coach McGuire's best friend is Jewish."

Sometimes, said Majerus, you have to bring in the ethnic thing. They can't afford to bring too many boys to campus, and those that Majerus does bring in—why, he wants everything in Marquette's favor. No sense in wasting expenses for a weekend.

Lee's practice was over and it was almost time for Majerus to leave. "What we'll do from now on," he said, "is send Jack Burke over a few times to the school just to let Butch know we're still interested in him. Then we might get a black player to write him a letter telling him how much of a family we are at Marquette."

But Majerus wanted Butch to visit Marquette after he had seen all the other colleges—"to make the final impression." He believed that Marquette had a decided advantage over some of the others. He explained that "of the top 120 kids in the country, 94 are probably black. So most coaches will go after the 26 white kids only. We go for the ones we think we can land."

Ultimately, Majerus left Clinton a happy man.

He began speaking quickly after a final few words with Lee, and he thought that maybe this was a prize he had landed: "I picked up the fact that he would like to leave New York. And he did say he'd visit us. You did hear him say that, didn't you? But I hope we're not hurt by the fact that he wants to play as a freshman. We can't guarantee that. But, geez, he's the best guard I've seen."

And so, on the basis of a few minutes of viewing time, Marquette offered Butch Lee a four-year ride. It was worth at least $12,000. And, who knows? Maybe millions before Butch called it a career in the pros.

So he accepted Marquette's offer. And for another year, Majerus found that his role at Marquette—perhaps his role in life—was justified.

Butch Lee got what he wanted too: a high-powered college that could showcase his skills and give him national exposure. Coach McGuire got another superstar to help him continue a winning tradition. And the hunter, Rick Majerus, got the ultimate prize —an inner-city kid with a suburban jump shot.

CHAPTER IV

Big, Big Man
on Campus

Power: It means winning in college athletics. Power: It means getting the top-ranked football player over to the Governor's Mansion to shoot a little pool. Power: It means getting Dean Rusk, the former Secretary of State, to write a letter to a high-school basketball hotshot.

Power begets power in big-time sports. There are fringe benefits that a football powerhouse can offer that are unmatched, at least unmatched by less powerful colleges—quality coaching, national exposure, "pro-type" experience, high-paying part-time and summertime jobs, and those valuable connections with old grads. In the end, that's why the big college—or, at least, the aggressive one—can catch the big athlete. It's why Colorado Mines rarely produces the All-American, but Notre Dame does.

And the big, strong, quality athlete? He wields his own sort of power: although he may be only seventeen years old, he can hold a college's athletic destiny in his strong right arm for four years and he can spend most of his senior year in high school taking junkets to campuses around the United States, sampling their wares. Often, he winds up writing his own ticket: he can tell athletic directors exactly what sort of job he wants for his father, what subjects he wants to study, what kind of car he wants to drive, what he will need in extra cash.

The college and the athlete need each other. The college has known this for a long time. The athlete, just a teen-ager, learns it very quickly. And it goes beyond cynicism—it is a way of life.

So the unending, frantic, ritualistic search by the colleges for the super athlete boils down to this, according to one super athlete, Rick Barry:

"People like to have winners. That's the American way."

The unanswered question (and usually the unasked one), though, is this: Is it the best way?

Reflecting on the question years too late to change anything, a dozen of America's most prized athletes all concede that too much emphasis was put on winning in the days when they were being heavily recruited. Yet, they all were part of a winning system. Some never knew what it was like to endure a losing season until they became pros. They had gone through grade school, junior high school, high school, and college as one-man shows—powerful enough to carry a team on their broad backs.

Although they all acknowledge that they had their pick of colleges, each one—from Ben Crenshaw, the golfer, to Julius Erving, the basketball wizard—says, curiously, that he heard of "someone else" getting the favors, "but not me." Curious, indeed. If you're not going to do favors for the super athlete, for whom would you do them?

Still, many of them do admit that a seventeen-year-old has an undue amount of pressure on him when he receives 100 scholarship offers. But they were well treated at college after they finally made the choice, their recruiters' promises were honored, and for each of them the college experience was positive. Of course, each was a superstar, so he had the absolutely enviable position that every red-blooded American boy dreams of: the world by the tail, cheering crowds, doting coaches, first class all the way.

For their classmates less endowed by nature or higher education, life in the late twentieth century might more nearly resemble the world described more than 300 years earlier by Thomas Hobbes: selfish, preying, nasty, brutish, and short. But for the young superman with the rifle arm, dead eye, or quick move, the world will beat a path to the doorstep.

And what are the perquisites of super-stardom?

"I had offers of everything from girls to wardrobes to freezers stocked with food," recalls Matt Snell, who chose Ohio State. Then he went on to become the New York Jets' top rusher, and one of the best in pro football.

He becomes nostalgic now when he recalls being wooed by the colleges, and by one in particular, "A beautiful school out West, with a green campus. I hadn't seen anything like it back home." Home was a poor neighborhood in Carle Place, Long Island, where seventy-five scholarship offers poured in.

His head was turning until his mother finally told him, "Look, if the coach is offering you something he can't put down on paper, forget it." So, says Snell, he went to Ohio State because "the only one who was straight with me was Coach Woody Hayes."

They were happy to have Snell, all right. One of the athletic directors even told him, "We want you to be a student first and an athlete second." That made Snell laugh.

"That sounds nice," he says. "But when an education is worth $20,000—well, you know they're going to get their money's worth." To Snell, it meant that in reality football had to come first. He felt an obligation to the team, because they were the reason he was at the college in the first place. Even though no one told him the football practices transcended study time, he just knew they did. It was an unspoken sort of pressure, and he accepted it as part of the system.

Naturally, the system provided him with goodies as well. Indeed, every top player at Ohio State—and probably at most other major colleges around the country—received batches of season tickets. In a sense, they became "legal scalpers." It was simple. "If you were a pretty good player, you could get an alumnus to take a ticket off your hands for $300," Snell remembers.

(*The New York Times*)

Woody Hayes, coach of Ohio State's football team, talks over old times with a distinguished alumnus who graduated from the system to the New York Jets, Matt Snell.

Everyone has heard of offers connected with big-time athletics at big colleges. But the system is so pervasive that it extends, believe it or not, to rodeo. Yes, rodeo. More than forty colleges in the United States give rodeo scholarships, and each cowboy college wants to be Number One as badly as Ohio State or U.C.L.A. or Notre Dame does.

Shawn Davis, a household name on the rodeo circuit, attended Montana State. He says that five colleges tampered with him while he was there. And one of them, Brigham Young, "offered me a full ride—money and jobs, too—if I left."

Rodeo athletes may be the only ones who admit they get paid for doing what they're doing as undergraduates. Phil Lyne, the top high-school rodeo phenomenon a few years ago, received half a dozen offers before settling down at Sam Houston State in Texas. However, he was allergic to the pine trees that dotted the campus; so he switched to Uvaldi Junior College.

There is prize money in intercollegiate rodeo. Lyne won as much as $200 a night in, for example, calf roping, a non-credit course. But he has no regrets that he finally dropped out. In 1972 he earned $84,000.

Another "rare" scholarship once sought out a hockey player, Ken Dryden, who went on to become perhaps the foremost goalie in the world. When he was making a name for himself as a high-school net-minder in Toronto, not many colleges across the border in the States were chasing him. Michigan Tech, however, was eagerly doing so.

Michigan Tech was the best in collegiate hockey at the time by virtue of its goal tending. And the best man on its team was none other than Tony Esposito, who became the modern-day holder of the single-season shutout record as a professional, and who (along with Dryden) ranked as one of the finest goalies in history. But Dryden now insists that Esposito was one of the things wrong with Michigan Tech, in addition to its scholastic program.

"Even if I had gone to the school," he speculates, "it

wouldn't have made much sense for me to sit on the sidelines while Tony played. That's what Tech must have figured was my reason for not going there. A few days after I spoke with them, and told them I really didn't care to go to the school, I got a last-ditch letter from the basketball coach."

Dryden was flabbergasted when he opened the letter—and saw that it offered him a basketball scholarship. The basketball coach was telling him that, look, we know you don't want to sit around for two years while Tony Esposito plays goalie. So why don't you play basketball for us for two years? Then Esposito will graduate, and we'll put you on the hockey team.

But it wasn't just the sports factories that were after Dryden. Princeton came courting, too—but he decided that he didn't like the Tiger, either. What turned him off was the freshman hockey coach.

"He didn't try to attract me to the school by saying nice things about Princeton," Dryden recalls, "but by saying negative things about all the other schools that wanted me. That wasn't my idea of what a coach or a college should be."

Finally, he chose Cornell, a happy choice as it turned out. He became an All-America, the university became the national champion in hockey, and he got an education. Eventually he went to law school while playing for the Montreal Canadiens.

One thing stands out in his recollections of recruiters: "They all started off their conversations with, 'How's your mom and dad?' "

Another prized teen-ager, this one farther south, remembers how the recruiters attempted to get on a boy's good side. "You're the type of kid I'd want my daughter to marry" was the line handed to Steve Spurrier.

Spurrier, later the quarterback for the San Francisco 49ers, was the epitome of the collegiate Golden Boy. He was invited to visit fifty colleges, he actually visited twelve of them, and he wound up at the University of Florida. He went there, he says, "because it was a good school, had a good schedule and good weather to throw the ball."

He was wooed by many colleges before he made his decision, however, and one of the most insistent wooers was Vanderbilt, in his home state of Tennessee.

"I flew up in the Governor's private helicopter in Nashville," recalls Spurrier. "Then I visited him in the Governor's Mansion and we shot some pool."

Spurrier was a celebrity in Florida, too, especially after he won the Heisman Trophy as the country's top college football player. He spent so much time on the banquet circuit, accepting more accolades, that he never got a degree. It wasn't that he was in academic trouble, he makes clear. It was just that he had to devote so much time to organizations wanting to honor him. But even if he had had academic difficulties, they wouldn't have presented any problem.

Spurrier explains: "We had a guy who's full-time in charge of seeing that players don't flunk out."

Governors don't invite tennis players over to shoot pool. Still, Sandy Mayer received offers from a hundred schools. One of those that extolled their tennis programs was Rice University, in Houston. Even today, Mayer fondly recalls his weekend there.

"I'd pay money just to have another one like that," he says. "They put on a fantastic show for me. As soon as I got off the plane, they talked a guy into moving out of his apartment and I got the nicest rooms on campus."

That night at a basketball game, one of the members of the tennis team motioned to the cheerleaders and asked Sandy, "Which one would you take if you had your choice?" Mayer picked the prettiest one and was told, "She's yours."

She accompanied him later to a "superparty." He remembers that "they had this fabulous apartment and they rented casino gambling equipment—it was fake money, but the top prize was a bottle of booze."

Mayer fell in love with the cheerleader. Suddenly, he couldn't make up his mind about college. He had always thought he'd go to Stanford; when it came to a tennis program and academics, he felt, it was superior to Rice.

"I felt a lot of pressure in making the decision," he says. "I was trying hard not to be swayed by the fact that I loved that girl."

It is unlikely that Rice's recruiters were omniscient and thus could foresee that Mayer would fall in love with a Rice cheerleader. But they certainly did know how to show him a good time—even though the N.C.A.A. rules do not permit colleges "or their agents" to take prospective athletes into gaming halls. But a private party? That was, apparently, a horse of a different color.

For weeks after his magic night, Mayer was confused. He sat around his home in Wayne, New Jersey, pining for the girl. Yet he was still attracted to Stanford. His father noticed all the mail coming from the girl, sized up the situation, and finally told him, "Make a rational decision."

He decided on Stanford instead of the girl and became the most acclaimed college tennis player in the United States. He won the National Collegiate title, was ranked in the top twenty nationally, and then left college to devote his full attention to tennis.

Mayer was outspoken even while a student. He later said, "I don't understand why so much emphasis is placed on athletics and why so many scholarships are given out. College shouldn't be the training ground for professional athletics."

However, he doesn't hold with the fashionable thesis that colleges are "exploiting" athletes. "That's a lot of bunk," he believes. "A lot of athletes are raping the colleges. You've put an athlete in an environment where there's a library. And there's all sorts of remedial help for him. If he doesn't take advantage of it, it's his fault—not the college's."

Few colleges were after Tom Seaver. He had a so-so reputation in high school. "I hope to tell you," he freely admitted later when asked if he could be considered a late bloomer. Now he is one of the best pitchers in baseball. But when he played at a junior college in Fresno, California, he had to call the University of Southern California. They didn't call him. He asked for a scholarship and was told, "We've got good reports on you, but we'd like to take a further look."

A further look to U.S.C. meant sending Seaver to Fairbanks, Alaska. A sort of scouting league was developed up there, where good young ballplayers could show their stuff far from the prying eyes of scouts for other colleges. In a sense, Seaver was having a tryout. He passed and got his U.S.C. scholarship.

Years later, when he was starring for the New York Mets, Seaver was asked by U.S.C. to visit a high-school player in Summit, New Jersey. He drove over from his home in Greenwich, Connecticut, and told the boy and his coach that U.S.C. was sensational in baseball, football, and basketball. Seaver learned that Gale Sayers had already beaten him to the youngster to say a few words for Sayers's alma mater, Kansas. Was the boy impressed with all this celebrity treatment?

"Evidently not," said Seaver. "He just signed up to go to Maryland."

Although Ben Crenshaw got thirty offers to play golf, he had an easy decision. He chose the University of Texas at Austin "because that's where my teaching pro lived." For Crenshaw, Texas was "a great academic school—plus they gave me a four-year scholarship and $145 a month for room and board."

During his first two years, he attended classes regularly. But his team won the N.C.A.A. championship, and more and more tournaments beckoned the squad in general and Crenshaw in particular. He had become a golfer and not a student.

"My last year there I wasn't actually in Austin," he admits. "I was invited to so many tournaments. I'd call back to Austin to people in my class and ask what to study. I did take books along. But I wasn't in the mood to study when I was someplace else."

When he had been on campus, Crenshaw put in "at least" four hours a day on the golf course. Finally, in his junior year, he decided to leave. He jumped to the pros as the most heralded collegian since Jack Nicklaus.

This cavalier attitude—apparently not caring whether an athlete graduates and, in fact, making it virtually impossible for him to devote time to academics—has prevailed at many colleges in the United States. But Jerry West, the Los Angeles Lakers star, says that he did not experience it at the University of West Virginia.

"When I was recruited—and I must have got at least a hundred letters—West Virginia made it a point that I would graduate," he says.

Many colleges "make it a point" that the athlete will graduate. Sal Bando, former Arizona State star now with the Oakland A's, recalls that "being on scholarship, and being known, helped cut a lot of corners. You were moved to the front. You never had to wait on line."

For Julius Erving, going to college also meant getting the right coach! "I heard about friends who didn't get along with their coach, and I wanted to make sure this didn't happen to me. I also heard about guys who were forgotten about as far as their education went. I was promised extra help if I needed it." He selected the University of Massachusetts, then quit for a six-figure pro basketball career and, after jumping some pro teams, wound up with the New York Nets.

What does all this coddling do to a boy's head—to anyone's head?

Rick Barry, the ex-Miami All-America and later all-star pro with the Golden State Warriors, says the superstar search "has gotten out of hand."

He recalls that Bruce Hale (his college coach and now his father-in-law) "catered to Rick Mount in Indiana. Bruce had always said he'd never run after a kid. But now it's at the point where you have to ingratiate yourself with these kids. And not only that, the parents get into the act."

Perhaps it all comes back to Barry's earlier statement—that

winning is the American way. Or Matt Snell's logic: "Schools are competing for a limited amount of talent and they have to use whatever lures are at their disposal. If you're a coach at a big school, you have to win."

Perhaps some colleges don't care what happens to the hero when his playing days are over. Perhaps they don't give them academic direction.

Take Shawn Davis, the rodeo star, who complains, "I ended up with the wrong kind of degree." He's got a B.A. in education from Western Montana.

Ask any college about its policies of wooing the super athlete and it is likely to pass the buck. But, says Jerry West, "Everyone goes out and does it. And they make excuses why they have to do it. But they do it."

How they do it could be an object lesson in motivation. A college might use a Secretary of State, or an astronaut, a singer perhaps, or a governor. It might even be a thoroughbred race horse—a Triple Crown winner is best. As long as the name has clout, many colleges prevail upon a celebrity to help recruit the blue-chip athlete.

But a horse?

"Secretariat is a Kentuckian all the way," says Coach Joe Hall, who guides the University of Kentucky's basketball team.

"We use Secretariat's name in recruiting quite a bit. He's an attraction around here. In fact, we use him in a lot of ways. When L.S.U. came in, he bit their center."

Over the years, the blue-chip player has heard from these notables, too:

Col. Frank Borman for West Point—"First, they ask me about being an astronaut."

Former Secretary of State Dean Rusk for Davidson—"We don't use him too much any more. Not too many kids know who he is today," says a school official.

Moses Gunn, the actor, for Grambling—"If not for athletics, I guess the school wouldn't be known at all."

Ex-Governor John J. McKeithen for Louisiana State University—"I went at it with everything I had. I must have entertained two dozen boys at the Governor's Mansion with milk and cookies."

Bing Crosby for Gonzaga—"When we wanted to encourage a kid, Bing would drop him a note; but we wouldn't bother with just anybody," says a school official.

This celebrity business is used by most colleges; that is, most of those that have a celebrity to use. Some of them, however, are leery of using the big name. The public information director for Alabama, Charles Thornton, explains why:

"It's a gray line as to what's legal. So we don't like our alumni to talk to a prospective student on his own. Once an alumnus goes to a boy, he's automatically representing the school. What if he starts entertaining the kid?

"Our policy is that the young man will be dealing with the coaching staff when he gets here. It has a phoniness about it—you know, using a show-biz personality or a politician. Most of them will get overzealous. Of course, we don't have to employ these names. Coach Bryant himself is a pretty good lure to come here."

"Using celebrities has a ring of phoniness," concurs Dave Levy, assistant athletic director at the University of Southern California—which never invokes the name of John Wayne and which apparently doesn't classify Tom Seaver strictly as a celebrity.

"For us to pull John Wayne out of a hat would be a false sort of recruiting," Levy says.

Another West Coast official says that the colleges that call on politicians and heroes "usually are one-university states, and having a good team in the college has a lot to do with the prestige of their state."

No one, though, would accuse Massachusetts of being a one-university state, and no one would accuse Harvard of being a football factory. But, an official of Notre Dame laments, "the

Kennedys stole a couple of good ballplayers away from us and sent them to Harvard."

Richie Szaro remembers scrimmaging on a field in the Greenpoint section of Brooklyn one day when Robert F. Kennedy came along and said hello. Szaro was the star of St. Francis Prep's football team then, in the mid-sixties.

Although Kennedy wasn't in Brooklyn on a football-scouting mission—he was campaigning for the Senate—he was well aware of Richie Szaro. "By the questions he asked me," Szaro recalls, "I guess he already knew something about me. He told me to drop over to his place sometime. Then he told me I should go to look at Harvard, and he told me what Harvard had to offer."

Harvard won a place in Szaro's heart—to the consternation of Notre Dame. "We thought," said the Notre Dame official, "that the boy really was coming here."

Except for utilizing former athletes to say a good word, Notre Dame hasn't employed celebrities in recruiting. "We've got the charisma of Notre Dame," explains Col. John Stephens, the assistant athletic director. "We just tell a boy, 'What school do you think of when you say football?' Notre Dame has to be in the first three."

But when high-school stars are wooed by Vanderbilt in Nashville, the assistant coaches make sure to take them to the Grand Ole Opry, the Pantheon of country music.

Vanderbilt's Number One fan is Jerry Reed, who made it to the top of the music charts with his song "When You're Hot You're Hot." The reason the college particularly loves Reed, explains a friend, is that he is "just a good ole country boy. Not one of those newer types. He's a sports-family man."

Sometimes the personalities resent being called upon. Recently, Bill Mazer, the television broadcaster, received a call from a Michigan official to talk to a high-school basketball player that Michigan was after.

"The kid's Jewish, isn't he?" Mazer asked the official.

"Well, yes," was the reply.

"And that's why you wanted me to talk to him, isn't it?" said Mazer. "If he were Italian, you wouldn't have called."

"Well, yes."

Mazer said he resented being used as window dressing.

More and more, ethnicity is being employed. Black athletes call other black athletes. Ex-Governor McKeithen of Louisiana concedes, "We've got problems from other states. They're luring our black athletes away from us. It's still a problem to convince our own blacks that they'll be well treated in our schools."

Syracuse, perhaps, is more diplomatic. "We've used Peter Falk," said a spokesman. "The boys we recruit are impressed with a position a gentleman holds in society, and maybe he can impart a philosophy, a bit of wisdom based on his experience in life." Syracuse, however, brings in a personality only "when we've identified a prospect as a superb one. You certainly don't want to trouble a man like Peter Falk with every Tom, Dick, and Harry."

According to Davidson officials, Dean Rusk, while he was Secretary of State, wrote several letters for the college and its basketball team, which was coached then by the redoubtable Lefty Driesell before he moved on to Maryland.

"I played basketball for Davidson," Rusk says, "and I used to watch the games when I had a chance. But honestly, I don't remember writing letters for the school."

That's not how a Davidson aide remembers it. He recalls that Rusk even wrote a few letters after Driesell left. But not lately.

One of the toughest recruiting jobs in recent years befell the armies of West Point graduates. The unpopularity of the Vietnam War, compounded by a five-year military obligation, left Army's football team decimated and turned away many of the best and brightest prospects.

Even Colonel Borman, the astronaut, conceded that "it's difficult" for those reasons. Still, he says, he speaks "to fifteen or twenty boys a year about going to the Point—and sometimes the coaching staff brings prospects over to my house when the team is down here in Miami."

(*The New York Times/Don Hogan Charles*)
Lew Alcindor of Power Memorial High in Manhattan fixes his eyes on
the future: U.C.L.A., the Milwaukee Bucks of the National Basketball
Association, fame and fortune as Kareem Abdul-Jabbar.

The most famous letter ever written on behalf of U.C.L.A. was sent by Ralph Bunche to a rather tall youngster in New York named Lew Alcindor. Bunche was one of a number of esteemed black graduates of the school who wrote to the seven-footer. Alcindor, of course, became a legend at the university, then changed his name to Kareem Abdul-Jabbar and became a legend in the pros.

These selling jobs are prevalent, but J. D. Morgan, the athletic director at U.C.L.A., says it doesn't have to be that way. "The way you recruit a youngster best," he says, "is to sell your institution as an educational institution—coupled with a particular athletic program. It's hard, detailed work. The other part—meeting people like Arthur Ashe and Rafer Johnson—that's just the glamour part."

It may be "the glamour part," but for many schools it's still the most important part: name-dropping into the world of the young and impressionable.

McKeithen is probably the most outspoken recruiter in the country. He enjoyed having his power as governor help him build up the football and basketball teams at Louisiana State.

"Why, I helped recruit the first black players there," he says. "Previously, it was a segregated school. I remember we had this one outstanding basketball prospect, Collis Temple, and I called him and spoke to his daddy, and his daddy, who was a school principal, said, 'Governor, if I let my boy go to L.S.U., will you see that he's not mistreated?' And I told his daddy that I'd treat the boy like my own son. And you know what? That boy became a credit to his school and to his people."

Then there was the high-school football All-America, Brad Davis, who couldn't make up his mind. The boy's parents wanted him to go to dental school.

"Well, I couldn't assure them he'd go to dental school," the governor remembers. "That's a violation. But I told them that we never had a man fail to go on to graduate school."

Another boy, Warren Capone, was thinking of going to Notre

Dame—"which was turning handsprings to get him," the governor says.

"I had him over to the Governor's Mansion for coffee and cake," he reports, as though rendering a State of the State message to the Legislature. "I invited them all to the Governor's Mansion. I'd ask them, 'Why do you want to leave Louisiana? You want to live someplace in Colorado or Indiana? How's your friends and family going to cheer for you there?' "

CHAPTER V

The Nouveau Riche

The good, rich citizens of Lafayette, Louisiana, had oil wells that were producing thousands of barrels a day. And in the middle of that black gold stood their college. Its name: the University of Southwestern Louisiana.

At the best cocktail parties, at formal dinners in high places, or out at Grosse Pointe, people somehow never got around to talking about Southwestern Louisiana. Its name was not household. This was a situation that could not continue, not when its followers and graduates were beginning to make their marks in the world. There was a certain respect lacking.

The outside world didn't know that Southwestern Louisiana was part of a handsome network of state colleges started by the Kingfish, Huey Long. Or that its academic program was respectable.

And so, in the 1960s, infusions of money from alumni and fans began pouring in. The college grew bigger. When that happens, the academic program sometimes grows a little smaller, and more and more of the money winds up in the hands of the athletic department instead of the chemistry department. But the result in this case was extraordinary: the college with no name became, by

1972, the fourth-ranked basketball power in the United States and reached the national collegiate quarter-finals.

The next year, it was suspended for 126 violations—the greatest number in the history of the National Collegiate Athletic Association.

"How was it possible?" asked alumni, faculty members, administrators, and townspeople. How, indeed. Yet, it wasn't an isolated case, in spite of its remarkable dimensions. Sports had become such a big business, and sports had helped make so many colleges "respectable," that in the last decade no-name schools suddenly sprouted into national prominence around the country.

"No one wants to be a light heavyweight," says Dr. Fred Miller, now athletic director at Arizona State University, but formerly at one of the famous "little big schools"—Long Beach State in California.

"A light heavyweight is too small for the big schools, too large for the little ones. So you wind up with an athletic program that's nowhere.

"To get big-time, there first has to be a desire to make it. The institution has to want to—and to decide how big. Then the alumni come into the picture. Once you determine how much backing you have, then you determine what you can sell to potential athletes. In Long Beach, we had the beach. We had to decide: Do we play Whittier, Occidental, Pomona—or do we play the major schools? A never-never land is a difficult place to be.

"And when you start winning, you start getting support, and you start getting more athletes. You keep score. It's more fun to win than to lose."

At Southwestern Louisiana, everyone was having fun—no matter what it cost. Toby Warren, who became athletic director after the deluge, remembers what it was like:

"Some of the students took tests for athletes. The students from up north would be given transportation back home for Thanksgiving and Christmas. The parents were flown in for the games. All of this was illegal."

Warren took over the post of athletic director late in 1973, after the basketball squad had been suspended from varsity play for two years, and *every other varsity sport* at the college had been placed on indefinite probation. In the three years leading up to the disciplinary bombshell, he says, Southwestern Louisiana's athletic program did not graduate one athlete.

"They weren't student-athletes," he says. "They were athletes."

Indeed they were. After basketball was dropped, the twelve players on basketball scholarships went to other colleges—and every one became a starter, even the twelfth man.

"There's been a void," Warren admits, glancing back at the college's brief career in the sun. "Basketball revenue meant about $150,000 a year to us—out of a $1.2 million budget."

"How do you pull a program together after it's been zapped?" Warren wonders. Perhaps it started with a whole new philosophy. When he got the job as A.D. (Athletic Director), he was twenty-eight years old. More surprisingly, his background was business. He was a management consultant in Chicago.

"You're going to see a business orientation more and more," he says. "When you've got athletic facilities worth from $10 million to $15 million, and you've got budgets for athletics as high as $3 million, then you've got to have financial people. I think this is a trend. Look at S.M.U.—they just hired an A.D. who was a stockbroker.

"The sooner universities understand that college athletics is big business, and they need businessmen running it, the better off they'll be."

Once he took over, he shocked just about everyone by announcing that every coach and official under contract had to agree that his job would be terminated if he were found in violation of N.C.A.A. rules. In addition, Warren had the same clause written into his own contract—only stronger. If any member of his department is in violation, Warren himself also will resign.

"Now the question is," Warren says, "how do we start from

the beginning? It took a whole re-education. There was an uneducated involvement regarding rules on the part of alumni and friends. That will stop. I've been communicating with more people —booster clubs, the local community, coaches, alumni. You know, I'm in weekly communication with Warren Brown over at the N.C.A.A. My coaches come to me with so many questions on rules.

"But education is the big thing. We tell the booster club people what they can do and can't do. We're surrounded by an oil community. People bought our athletes shoes and coats and other things. We have to explain to them that if they contact a kid and talk about our school, they're acting as a representative of the university. They were doing this on their own sometimes and the athletic department didn't even know about it. Now, we've got to stop them from being so eager."

This fresh start he likens to "walking on eggs." But, he says, "We'll be damned if we do it again, the old mistakes, after what we went through. We've got a new head football coach, a new basketball coach, a new athletic director."

Southwestern Louisiana may rise again. Even as Warren wrung his hands over past abuses, his basketball coach, Jim Hatfield, planned for the college's return to the big time in 1975, including games in the Louisiana Superdome against California-Berkeley and Washington State.

"Our prestige and programs in the past enabled us to get a top schedule," concedes Warren. "The fact that our program in the past had a lot of cheating in it didn't affect our future. That national image still remains in the eyes of kids in New York, Boston, Birmingham, or Houston. And if they're super players and they see we have a super reputation, why they'll think this is a school that can make it to the top."

Since the old, illegal lures aren't there any more, what inducements are there to attend Southwestern Louisiana?

"Realistically, why would a kid come from New York, say, to play at Southwestern Louisiana? The only way is if the kid falls in love with the coach. Of course there's another way—if the kid is enticed by things that the regulations don't allow. But our recruiters will talk to a friend of the athlete. Usually, there's one around who acts as his agent. The parents of poor black kids usually are not involved, and neither is his coach. What we find with these ghetto kids is some big-brother type who takes care of him, and the kid respects him. The big brother is the one we go after. The big brother is told that if the boy is a legit pro prospect, he might have a chance to represent him. And anyway, he's given tickets to games in his area."

In 1974 Southwestern Louisiana which was prohibited from playing, signed six basketball players who were red-shirted. That is, they received athletic scholarships, went to classes for the year, but still had four years of varsity eligibility remaining. The term "red shirt" stems from the fact that players who were being held out for a year, and weren't playing varsity ball, would wear red shirts during scrimmages. You didn't hit them quite so hard.

While the Raging Cajuns' basketball program was in limbo, its football program, predictably, collapsed. In 1973, its first year of "indefinite probation," the squad posted an 0–10 mark. But Warren remains optimistic.

"We're looking over our 1980 schedule," he says, "and we're talking to Syracuse, Penn, Florida State."

Finally, Warren concedes, "if it takes what it used to take to win—we won't be winning. We just can't afford to screw up."

But if Southwestern Louisiana was the dubious record holder, Long Beach State received more national exposure for its violations, which resulted in 1974 in the college's being placed on a three-year probation.

Even now, though, the coach who brought Long Beach to the sports pages of America—Jerry Tarkanian—recalls the years of ascendancy fondly and without bitterness. He was perhaps like Browning's classic hero—he attempted to take the main chance, rather than gathering his pennies one by one.

"The best way to play the big schools is to lose," he says. "Once you lose, they'll want to play you."

His dilemma: how to win and still get the big schools to play.

Long Beach State was one of those pretty, anonymous colleges that were a part of the mushrooming California university system. It had almost 30,000 students by the late 1960s. But the average age of the students was twenty-four. Half of them were married. Clearly, there wasn't much of a rah-rah spirit around, not when people had to worry about going to a job or taking care of a family.

"Where do you want to go?" Dr. Fred Miller asked school officials in 1966, when he took over as athletic director. They said that they wanted to make a name for themselves. The problem was that there were comparatively few alumni (the school had opened in 1949) and only limited financial backing.

"If you can catch fire with an athletic program, the effect on school spirit is tremendous," says Dr. Miller. "Take City College of New York, a commuter school. Remember when they won the basketball Grand Slam in 1950? Spirit is what holds a school together—it's not going to be a book of poetry."

Enter Tarkanian, and a supporting actor, Jim Stangeland, football coach.

"Who cared? I cared," says Tarkanian. "They gave me a recruiting budget for my first year of $100. The community of Long Beach didn't care."

Tarkanian came up from the ranks of the junior colleges, where he had established himself as the best in the West. His teams won J.C. championships every year. And that is how he began to build Long Beach State—on junior college transfers. Three years in a row he landed the J.C. player of the year.

Some of the players got into college, the N.C.A.A. discovered later, because other students took tests for them. Others got apartments rent-free, and at least one had a motel room for himself and his girl friend for two weeks.

These extras, along with Tarkanian's evangelical approach, helped him recruit black ghetto stars and turn them into finished basketball players.

Part of his spiel to land players was the terrain—the beach. "You plugged what you had," explains Dr. Miller. Later, it would be the liner *Queen Mary*, which was tied up at the Long Beach docks.

Among the stars Tarkanian wooed and won was Ed Ratleff, one of the greatest teen-agers in the country. Soon, Long Beach State was winning, and other colleges were noticing them. At the beginning, austerity was the rule. The team traveled to games in the players' cars. Once, a player's fan belt broke down as he was driving several other players to a game. The school refused to reimburse him.

In his first year, Tarkanian amassed a 20-6 record and, to his chagrin, "Some schools we were supposed to play dropped out after I got to Long Beach. They saw who I signed for the future."

This is an essential part of big-time basketball, and it points up why it is so difficult for a small college to make it. There are other serious problems. Says Tarkanian:

"The major schools won't play any place but at their place. You've got to play on the road if you're just beginning. We called that paying our dues. We traveled to Texas Tech, Houston, Marquette, Kansas. You see, the secret in big-time basketball is to play as many home games as possible."

This is a fact that many fans don't realize. In football, a team plays as many away games as home games. But in basketball, except for conference games, a team can call its shots. If you're U.C.L.A., you tell the other teams that they must play you at your home. Unless, of course, an extra-large, neutral arena is after you and can promise an extra-large fee.

Despite success, Tarkanian's teams couldn't sell tickets at home. During his reign, the college never sold more than 1,200 student tickets for a 12,000-seat arena. He didn't have much money to offer visiting colleges, so he wound up picking on the leavings of U.C.L.A.

He'd call up a college that was visiting U.C.L.A. for, say, $5,000 and tell the A.D., "Look, since you're going to be in the neighborhood anyway, why don't you play us for $1,500?"

Sometimes it worked. But once in a while he would get this reply: "Tark, how could I play you? If we lose, how can I explain to my alumni who Long Beach State is?"

On the other hand, he knew that to recruit the best players, he had to play the big schools. His players, meanwhile, were cajoled and conned into winning. Not enough money for steaks before a game? Tarkanian told them hamburger was healthier, that sirloin "curdled in the stomach."

"I'll bet there's never been a team before that made it to the top 10 on hamburgers," Tarkanian says.

"There's only about 100 schools in the country that have a continuity of funding," explains Dr. Miller. "Schools like Ohio State, Michigan State. So most schools have the problem. They can't make it in the big-time without funding, and they can't stay there without funding continuing."

How to make it? "You set up sports groups and you drum up support," says Dr. Miller. "You go to the community and tell them a winning team is good for the community." But, acknowledging the difficulties involved, he estimates that, in the two decades starting with 1950, only two relatively unknown colleges cracked the top 20 in football—Houston and Arizona State. "Football is a long haul in building a reputation," he explains, "but in basketball you need only one or two standouts."

By 1972, even after Long Beach had made it to the top four in national ranking and had come within one point of upsetting U.C.L.A. in the national championship tournament, the college's recruiting budget was under $3,000. It was going to be raised to $7,500 in 1973, but Tarkanian quit and switched to an unknown —the University of Nevada at Las Vegas. The cynical believed that he left because he saw N.C.A.A. handwriting on the court— he knew, they said, that an investigation was coming. Some months later, Jim Stangeland left as football coach, saying, "I promised my wife two years ago I'd go into private business." And a few months after that, the N.C.A.A. cracked down hard on the college, putting it on a three-year probation after finding dozens of violations.

"The N.C.A.A. coming into Long Beach," said Stangeland, "is like the United Nations marching on Poland for not fighting fair against Germany in World War II."

"It's a sad part of your life to see something collapse," says Dr. Miller. "But what concerned me about the whole thing was due process. The accused never faced the accusers. Now we must make sure the coaches understand the rules. Have you ever looked at the book of rules? It's a big one. But the reason rules are put in is to shore up the loopholes that everyone—except 1 percent—of the schools use."

Tarkanian now is content at Las Vegas. "I had a lot of administrative red tape at Long Beach," he explains. "Here we have a lot of people interested—the governor, a senator. And we have some plusses here to offer a boy. He can come here and see the bright lights. They see Lake Mead, one of the finest lakes in the world. It's a fun town to visit. But there's also some drawbacks in recruiting. We have some parents who just don't want their kids to go to Vegas."

He started at Vegas with a recruiting budget of $15,000. The state ranks first in the country in per capita aid to education. It has only one college in the city and only two in the state, and, in a sense, the state and all its inhabitants are pulling for it. The 6,200-seat Convention Center is sold out, although the college has only 6,500 students. ("The community wants a winner," says Tarkanian.)

While Long Beach was feeling its growing pains, the University of Texas, El Paso, was flexing its muscles. It recruited a host of ghetto youngsters from the East and, unbelievably, won a national championship in 1966.

It was uncharitably said of the players that they were able to do everything with a basketball except sign their names to it. Who cared? UTEP was on top.

"All anybody ever talked about was the team," says a member of the college's athletic department. "The economy of the city just hummed when we won. We've got a little bitty crackerbox gym; we sell 2,000 tickets, and they're gone the first day they're put on sale. We don't allow season ticket holders to keep their seats year to year. We want to spread them around. So every year, the first day, they're gone. And we still get a waiting list of a thousand names hoping something comes up during the season."

Still, it remains a tough job to bring players to El Paso. "You bring a super here and he says, my God, I just came from three schools and they have 15,000 seats. We have, well we say we have, 5,000 seats. But that's exaggerated. We're planning to build a new arena with 12,500 seats."

There are lures, though. "The weather has something to do with it. In December it'll be 65 to 75 degrees, and that's something a kid from New York or Detroit is interested in. We also tell them we're near a foreign country, which we are. Not far from the Mexican border, and that has a sort of exotic ring to it."

When it began, UTEP had to go the route of other unknowns —play on the road, at the homes of top-ranked colleges. "We did that a lot more than now," says the official. Now, apparently, other colleges trying to make reputations know they must face El Paso and are willing to play there.

The college plays in the Western Athletic Conference ("It's what you'd call a basketball conference"), but also received national acclaim for its track team. There's an easy explanation for that:

"Weather's the Number One factor to track people. Also we've got a good track facility. Our old football stadium is used exclusively for track. It holds 11,000 people, we've got runways, a Tartan track good for all weather."

After taking the basketball title in 1966, UTEP was criticized for allegedly not graduating its students and for being interested only in their four years of athletic eligibility. These criticisms hurt the college; so it upgraded its academic program. According to the official, however, the criticisms were not justified. "We graduated eight players on that championship team," he says.

After the big crackdown on certain colleges, many of them

small-time schools that had suddenly become big-time, the whole recruiting system came in for scrutiny.

Warren, the A.D. at Southwestern Louisiana, says, "When I talk to other A.D.'s, the subject of recruiting cheating doesn't seem to come up. I just assume that if their program's successful, they've been doing it."

Gary Colson of Pepperdine adds, "I don't think you can win big without cheating."

Abe Lemons of Pan American University says, "The only answer is to give every coach a lie-detector test. They could never publish the results. Lordy, it would blow the lid off."

CHAPTER VI

The All-American Rip-Off

"It goes deep, the corruption," said Myles Dorch, his voice almost a wail, "So far back. A kid can't even read, they'll let him play high-school basketball."

Myles Dorch knows first-hand about the tangled world of reading and rebounding. Before becoming a social worker, he played tough basketball himself at Cardinal Hayes High School in the Bronx, he was recruited into college ball, he spent four years in the early sixties at St. Anselm's in New Hampshire—and he even got the education and the degree he wanted.

But, as far as he could see, that put him ahead of the game. It put him ahead of other recruits, for example, who wound up with neither education nor degree, nor with the almighty career in the pros. It probably put him ahead of many truly hot basketball players who had difficulty reading a newspaper.

"It's the coaches," Dorch was saying, surveying the scene from his vantage point as a veteran of the system who now was trying to teach heavily recruited young athletes to avoid academic bankruptcy.

"The coaches," he said, "don't give a damn, and neither do the schools. No guidance. No relationship except three to five o'clock in the gym, and games. Don't worry about going to class, we'll fix you up. Just pad their grades, and push 'em right on out."

The corruption, he said, carries over onto the college scene: "I know of five kids right now in top-ranked colleges playing basketball who didn't graduate from high school."

According to educators like Dr. Roscoe C. Brown, Jr., the predominance of black athletes (64 percent in professional basketball) results not from any natural superiority but from "the disproportionate amount of energy" spent in the ghetto developing sports skills.

"What we need is balance," said Dr. Brown, director of New York University's Institute for Afro-American Affairs. "We need more education. Black youngsters pour too much time and energy into sports. They're deluded and seduced by the athletic flesh peddlers, they're used for public amusement—and discarded."

In Dr. Brown's view, most blacks find neither social mobility, educational fulfillment, nor financial success through what he calls "the mirage" of sports recruiting. For every Walt Frazier, posing next to his $30,000 Rolls-Royce, thousands of basketball prospects are rejected.

"Most of them are left without the skills needed for servicing or enriching the community," he concluded, "and that's the rip-off."

Translating his indictment of the system into raw statistics: for the 200,000 high-school seniors playing basketball each year in America's 22,000 public and private secondary schools, the odds against making the pros are astronomical, something like this:

Schoolboy seniors	200,000
College seniors	5,700
Drafted by the pros	211
Signed by the pros	55

This works out to about 1 percent of all college basketball players who reach the pro ranks, meaning that 99 percent don't even make it from the college level. But few youngsters or parents seem aware of the odds, especially after listening to the siren songs of the recruiters. And so the recruiting game goes on, and on.

It starts in junior high school, back in the rancid poverty of the ghettos where winos and junkies rot and where toddlers call out to dead rats, "Here, kitty."

Day and night, the young basketball dreamers escape to the asphalt courts to ply their trade—and wait for the offers. Sooner or later, usually sooner, grown men with names like Uncle Harry, Spook, and Big Bob move in. A free dinner here, and a promise there, and it starts.

"At that age," noted Myles Dorch, "two or three dollars is a lot of money. They think, 'Damn, somebody is *doing* something for me. This is great.' They don't realize that they're getting ripped off."

A few of the dreamers, of course, hit it big: a Tiny Archibald, celebrated superstar in the pros; an Adrian Dantley, who was promised the world as a high-school senior in Washington, D.C., and who advanced his dream by playing varsity ball as a freshman for Notre Dame; a Butch Lee, sorting out those offers from the 300 pursuing colleges.

For most, though, the gold-paved boulevard leading to professional wealth and glory turns out to be a dead end. No Rolls-Royce, no high-powered agent, no degree in history.

"You don't like to keep a boy's dream away from him," Dorch reasoned, "but you have to give him a sense of values."

One of the critical problems, he said, is that many of the recruits being pursued by the college talent scouts are functionally illiterate when they come out of high school: "They're given big money to play basketball, but they're not given the guidance to get an education. There's got to be something wrong with the system."

The problem is compounded by the use of junior colleges as "farm clubs" for the major college teams, and Dorch cites the case of Rudy Jackson to illustrate. Jackson played basketball for Bowne High School in Flushing, Queens, and then hurried off, in 1972, to Hutchinson Junior College in Kansas.

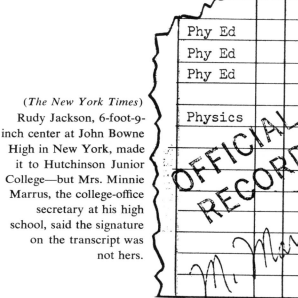

(The New York Times) Rudy Jackson, 6-foot-9-inch center at John Bowne High in New York, made it to Hutchinson Junior College—but Mrs. Minnie Marrus, the college-office secretary at his high school, said the signature on the transcript was not hers.

The only catch was that Jackson hadn't graduated from Bowne. But wait: no real problem. A transcript was forged. According to the athletic director at Hutchinson, it carried the high school's official seal. Result: a two-year probation for Wichita State University, which had "encouraged" Jackson to attend the junior college.

"They send kids to junior college to get their grades together," Dorch said, "and the junior college fixes them up. Lets them take their own equivalency tests, things like that."

Lou Carnesecca went the coaching route from St. John's University to the New York Nets of the American Basketball Association to St. John's again. He saw how the system worked at all levels: "Recruiting has gone from the back room to the living room in the last few years. It's more open now. There's more talk of cars, apartments, and other extras."

Dorch, an alumnus of the system, got his free steak dinners and his athletic scholarship, but he also got an education. So he survived the system. He then leaped clear of it by going to work for the Department of Social Services in New York City and a community center in the Bronx, where his goal was to keep a new generation of hotshots from making the same mistakes that some of his friends had made. Hotshots like old Larry, who was wined and dined in high school by the same recruiters, but who was too willing to head West for a promise.

"At college," Dorch remembered, "I heard about Larry out in New Mexico getting a free car; he racked it up, just playing ball. He stayed a year or two and just left. It didn't work out."

Another group of Dorch's friends trooped to a college in Texas after a recruiter told them, "You boys can come on down and play basketball—and if you're lucky, you can get an education." Dorch said the sales pitch turned him off. What happened to his friends? "None of those nine kids graduated, and only two got pro contracts."

Then there was Buster, so good that as a high-school sophomore he was getting $15 a game playing out of town, under a fictitious name, for a semi-pro team called the Harlem Astronauts. But Buster never reached the junior year and ended up hustling in the neighborhood trying to scratch out a living. The Pied Piper had led him on and left him.

"It's hard to get a good, secure job without a degree," Dorch said. "Most of the guys I played basketball with in school never got degrees. When their time was up, they're washed up."

What is needed, some community leaders feel, is a realistic approach: let the superstars "make it" if they can, but concentrate on the average youngsters instead.

"The new revolution is, you've got to invest in the kids," said Bob Williams, the unsalaried director of The Sports Foundation, a youth group whose programs include the annual Harlem Junior Olympics. "We want the pro stars to 'come back' and re-invest in the community."

Street scene: Spellbound spectators in Harlem watch as the Rucker summer tournament brings a touch of basketball glamour to the playground, and a chance for teen-agers to perform before college and pro scouts.

The flesh peddlers don't bother Williams, a former basketball player at New York University and a onetime coach.

"I went through the whole thing, too," he said. "Sought after, and all that. I've dealt with the flesh peddlers, I know 'em, some of 'em are my friends. But I look 'em straight in the eye and say, 'Don't rip off our kids anymore.' "

What does bother Williams is the lack of academic guidance for recruited athletes by school administrators, and especially coaches.

"We're not against athletic scholarships," he said. "We'd just like to see some academic 'insurance policies' in those scholarships."

In some cases, the easy road to recruiting leads to limbo. Cyril Baptiste, a heavily recruited Miami schoolboy, played four years of brilliant basketball for Creighton University in Nebraska.

REPORT CARD ON THE PROS—1974
(*Who Got Degrees and Who Didn't*)

NATIONAL BASKETBALL ASSOCIATION

	Yes	No
Atlanta Hawks	8	4
Boston Celtics	9	3
Buffalo Braves	10	2
Capital Bullets	8	4
Chicago Bulls	8	3
Cleveland Cavaliers	8	4
Detroit Pistons	8	4
Golden State Warriors	8	3
Houston Rockets	7	4
Kansas City-Omaha Kings	2	10
Los Angeles Lakers	10	2
Milwaukee Bucks	5	6
New York Knicks	8	5
Philadelphia 76ers	8	3
Phoenix Suns	9	3
Portland Trail Blazers	9	3
Seattle SuperSonics	4	8
Total	129	71

AMERICAN BASKETBALL ASSOCIATION

	Yes	No
Carolina Cougars	9	2
Denver Rockets	6	4
Indiana Pacers	5	6
Kentucky Colonels	7	4
Memphis Tams	5	5
New York Nets	4	7
San Antonio Spurs	4	7
San Diego Conquistadors	6	3
Utah Stars	7	3
Virginia Squires	9	1
Total	62	42

He reportedly went to class only rarely and eventually developed a drug habit that landed him in jail. Later, he tried to put the pieces of his life back together—playing in a minor league and trying not to think about the six-figure professional contract that he had lost along the way.

But these are the losers, right? How about the winners—the basketball players who survive with all kinds of flourishes and graduate to the pros? They may not all strike it rich, and they may not all stick around long enough to carve out great careers. But don't they at least have their college educations to fall back on?

Graduate—that may be the key word in evaluating the results of the system. If an athlete goes through college, he is supposedly no worse off than his classmate who majored in liberal arts instead of basketball. But before he can ever enjoy the full rewards of those four years on the campus, he presumably should "graduate" to something other than the pros. Maybe just graduate.

But even at a time when high-school athletes are being attracted into college and are being virtually assured of a diploma, about 63 percent of those in the professional basketball leagues in 1974 had received their college degrees. (See Tables page 81.) Of the 200 players on the 17 teams in the National Basketball Association, 129 had graduated and 71 had not. Of the 104 players on the 10 teams in the American Basketball Association, 62 had received their degrees and 42 had not.

None of the 27 teams scored 100 percent in the graduation test; that is, none was manned entirely by college graduates. The Virginia Squires of the A.B.A. came the closest: 9 alumni and 1 dropout. At the other end of the academic spectrum, the Kansas City-Omaha Kings listed 2 graduates and 10 dropouts. Even the New York Knicks, the "intelligentsia" of pro ball—with a Rhodes Scholar (Bill Bradley) and a mental gymnast (Jerry Lucas) on the roster—showed 5 college dropouts on a 13-man squad.

The figures do not necessarily reflect on the mental ability of the players; like people in any profession, they range from ordinary to brilliant. However, the figures do point up the fact that college basketball, in a gradual shift to big business, has grown into a farm system for the pros, in the same way that the junior colleges have grown into a farm system for the senior colleges.

The shift has become less gradual and more headlong in recent years because of the strong pull of, in one word, money. With the emergence of the rival A.B.A. to challenge the established N.B.A. for the talent available, a full war broke out between the two leagues and the chief weapon was money. At the same time, the lure of big-money contracts proved irresistible to many twenty-one-year-old ballplayers. It turned their heads away from the classrooms and toward the basketball courts, and greatly increased their concentration on impressing the pro scouts.

"After my junior year," said John Gianelli, an engineering student at the University of the Pacific before he signed with the Knicks, "I lost interest in school. I thought I had a future in pro ball. I hoped to sign a good contract. A good three-year contract in pro basketball is better than the money you can earn in ten to fifteen years at a steady job."

Steve Spurrier, the quarterback for the San Francisco 49ers in the National Football League, found the same sort of distraction. So, he also chose money instead of a degree from the University of Florida, where he had created personal and athletic legends as the undergraduate who could do it all.

"I needed a few credits for my degree in physical education when I left school," Spurrier said. "What good would a phys-ed degree have done me—allowed me to teach high-school football?"

Bill Bradley, who not only attended Princeton and Oxford but excelled in his studies at both universities, found plenty of things wrong with the pro system, even though he managed to combine it with an extraordinary academic career. In fact, after graduating from Princeton, he made the pros wait until he had come home from Europe. Then he launched his basketball career with the Knicks.

"College basketball and football should exist on a semipro level," he suggested, taking to the soapbox that will probably lead him into a political career when his sports whirl is over. "Athletes should be paid to play for a university in exchange for either money or their education. The choice should be left to the athlete.

"Actually, the recruiting by college basketball and football is all part of a minor-league system and should be considered that way. The pros should finance them."

Otherwise, Bradley feels, the supercharged pace of recruiting exploits young men and leads to a misplaced sense of values in the athlete and in the administration of the college.

To Rick Barry, one of the most traveled and most talented of the basketball pros, the crux of the matter is the college degree itself.

"There are no guarantees of making the pros or staying there," said Barry, who graduated from Miami before heading with his lawyer into the major leagues of basketball. "The degree is something to fall back on. College is a place for an education, not a training ground for the pros. If it's a minor league for the pros, let's specify it and pay athletes and give out certificates that they attended basketball practice."

College athletes, primarily basketball players, often complain that their practice sessions and travel schedules take them away from their studies too much of the time. Barry admits that in his final semester, because of travel and postseason tournament play, he attended only twenty-eight days of classes.

"That's not an excuse for not getting a degree, though," he said, generalizing the problem. "The teachers were understanding and I took my books and notes on the road. The lowest grade I got was 'C'; the rest were 'A's.' "

Henry Bibby received degrees in sociology and physical education at U.C.L.A., turned pro with the Knicks, and now agrees with Barry's estimate of the values involved.

"I don't buy this garbage that you can't study in season," he insisted. "U.C.L.A. provided plenty of tutors and people always wanted to help the athletes. That's what school is all about. You go for an education. How many guys make it to the pros? I went to college with the idea of making a living with my degrees. Pro basketball was the bonus."

Dean Meminger turned pro with the Knicks, then went back to Marquette for his degrees in sociology and philosophy. He later reflected: "A college degree doesn't really prepare you for anything, but it was important for me to become the only child in my family to get one. All black parents want an education for their kids. They feel an education is instrumental in helping solve some of the pursuits of black people—namely, equality.

"But college basketball in reality is pro basketball disguised as amateurism. I was a pro when I was fourteen years old and Rice High School recruited me. They gave me tuition, room, and board."

Dick Barnett played thirteen seasons in the N.B.A. before he retired to become an assistant coach with the Knicks. He had left Tennessee State without his degree, but since then has received his bachelor's and master's degrees and has kept studying toward his doctorate.

"Your values change as you get older," Barnett says. "You crave for the knowledge you let slip by in your younger days. A school should be responsible for an athlete's getting his degree, even if it means continuing his scholarship into his fifth year. After all, he was brought there to help the school with his athletic ability, and they owe him something in return."

Yet, for every scholar-athlete like Barnett or Bradley or Bibby or Meminger, there are a hundred others who get lost in the maze of temptations and rewards for just being twenty-one and strong.

"This is my record," Rod Thomas confessed after one of the most remarkable careers in college sports. "From 1955 to 1962, I played football—either in a game or in practice—at five colleges. I turned down a generous offer from still another school. And during those seven years, I also tried out with a professional team, coached a semipro team, and coached and taught at two prep schools.

"At no time did I use any name but my own, yet the National Collegiate Athletic Association and the colleges I played for never once caught me in my illegal activities. Not one, in fact, showed much interest in checking up on me as long as I could play football. I didn't start out with the intention of being an itinerant college athlete—it just happened that way. And the more it happened, the easier it became. I discovered that as long as I was a producing athlete, there was always someone to stake me and give me a fresh start when I grew restless."

Thomas had a lot more going for him than most tramp athletes. He went to one of the best prep schools in the South, the Castle Heights Military Academy in Lebanon, Tennessee. He was twice chosen the school's outstanding athlete. He was elected captain of the varsity football, basketball, baseball, and track teams. He also was a member of the student council. But before he graduated, he had offers from Georgia Tech, Tennessee, Indiana, Kentucky, Memphis State, and "any number of smaller colleges" —for football, not student council. However, he chose Vanderbilt, even though Memphis State kept writing him letters to this effect: "Let us know if you get unhappy or dissatisfied. We'll find a place for you here."

Halfway through his freshman football season, he dropped out of Vanderbilt and obligingly switched to Memphis State. The next summer, he left Memphis State and transferred to Compton Junior College, which had the added draw of being situated in California not far from Hollywood. He later migrated to Kansas State and to San Jose State. In all of these colleges, he was on scholarship.

Later, he looked back on it all and decided that it had been a merry-go-round that never really reached any destination—either athletically or academically. He may not have been "ripped off"; in fact, the colleges probably felt that he had done most of the "ripping off." But to Rod Thomas, football player extraordinaire, it still bore little relationship to life outside the good, gray walls of the universities.

"That's all part of a past," he theorizes, "that seems as unreal to me now as a chapter in an F. Scott Fitzgerald book."

CHAPTER VII

How to Succeed in Business

"If you want a winning team," a visiting rival tells the hockey coach at a college in the Midwest, "you'd better build some dorms and fill 'em up with booze and broads—like we did."

"If you don't fly," a football coach in the South observes, referring to airborne recruiting techniques, "you die."

"We tell our people," says the athletic director at the University of Tennessee, "as long as you support us, we're going to have the best sports program possible. Of course, if we start operating in the red, we'd have to tighten our belts and do without things."

The message, at least, is clear even if the words are different: in big-time college sports, solvency and survival are linked to victory.

Some colleges continue to make it, even with all the tightening pressures of inflation and backlash. And in their field houses, subsidized athletes operate out of locker rooms with luxurious red carpeting, closed-circuit television, quadrasonic sound for the stereo systems, and director's chairs displaying the names of the gladiators. But other colleges, in increasing numbers, are reassessing the situation because the dollars are no longer there. Still others, beneath the roar of the capacity crowds and the rush to na-

tional championships, are growing sensitive to all the pressures
—financial and academic—and are finally asking: "What price
victory?"

On the "plus" side for the major colleges: television revenue
has climbed—soared, in some cases, with the twin opportunities of
"Game of the Week" exposure and the postseason bowl games. On
the "minus" side: expenses have been climbing faster than revenue
at most colleges. The result: a kind of economic goal-line stand for
all colleges, regardless of opportunity or philosophy.

Though inflation isn't always the major problem, it still ranks
as the most obvious and the most pressing: $6,000 for the 100
dozen hockey sticks needed by a major college's varsity-freshman-
jayvee program; $50 a dozen for new Louisville Slugger baseball
bats, and about 25 dozen are required for a season; $20 a pair for
spiked baseball shoes, going to $25; 6 dozen oranges, at $1.20 and
up a dozen, to be quartered, iced, and brought onto the field at a
typical dual track meet.

Some colleges weather the storm, like the University of Tennessee—where the athletic budget exceeds $3 million and where
fans think nothing of driving 200 miles to watch their beloved
Volunteers play football. Bob Woodruff, the athletic director,
translates the signs positively: "The general public wants athletics
at every level. Our students, alumni, and faculty want it, too."

Despite its $3-million budget—more than the combined total
of the state's fourteen other publicly supported colleges and universities—Tennessee still shows a profit on athletics. Most colleges, though, don't. They don't, in spite of the fact that sports
attendance and income at a majority of the nation's 1,120 four-
year "team" colleges are at record levels. Penn State, for example,
took $500,000 out of the 1974 Orange Bowl; Notre Dame got
$420,000 for its Sugar Bowl appearance.

But even affluent colleges like Harvard, which has an endowment of $1.4 *billion* and a relatively antiseptic recruiting pol-
icy, are feeling the pinch. Though it offers no athletic scholarships

and prohibits its coaches from making recruiting trips, Harvard spends more than $7,500 a year on adhesive tape alone.

Harvard's Department of Athletics operates its own laundry, where 2,000 or more towels a day are washed. Like many other colleges, it has been forced to apply the old do-or-die college spirit to its helmets, shoulder pads, jerseys, and other equipment: everything gets handed down from varsity (after two or three seasons) to freshman teams, then to junior varsity and, finally, to the intramural squads. A repairman works full time patching up the equipment.

"Unless you have a winner, you're in bad shape," says Paul Prpish, athletic business manager at Marquette, whose nationally prominent basketball teams generate "substantial surplus revenue" for the college in Milwaukee.

But to get, and keep, a winner—there's the rub. That takes attitude, from the board of regents down through the ranks; and it takes a willingness to spend for talent, perhaps $75,000 and more for recruiting, or $500,000 a year for scholarships, as at the University of California, Los Angeles. And far greater amounts are often hidden under other headings in the budgets of some colleges.

"It's a national disgrace," complains Maurice Mitchell, chancellor of the University of Denver. "Students are becoming more critical about the cost of the big-time sports programs."

In desperation, the have-not colleges frequently seek a lower level of competition, which is one way to stay in the sports business without going broke. But the pressures of fielding a representative team still crowd most colleges of all sizes, big or small or inbetween.

Brown University, a relatively "pure" Ivy League college with an annual sports deficit of $650,000, fired its hockey coach in midseason in 1974 for what the athletic director called "loss of control over the players." The team had a record of 5 won and 10 lost. The deposed coach, Al Soares, insisted he had been told: "Listen, Al, it's the W's and L's that count. I'm sorry." Al was sorry, too.

Athletic budgets of $2 million or $3 million are not unusual at major colleges, and a few of the super powers like Michigan have reached the $4-million plateau, if it is a plateau. Despite an average football attendance of 85,000, an increase in ticket prices to $7, and heavy television revenue, Michigan says it nets only $100,000.

At the University of Colorado, whose gung-ho Flatiron Club financed a new $575,000 press box for the football stadium, the athletic budget for a typical year showed income of $2,241,900 and outgo of $2,264,300. The overhead, which included $335,600 for coaching salaries and $507,300 for athletic scholarships, listed only $70,800 for recruiting. But it carried $138,400 under the puzzling heading of "office expenses." (See Table, page 91.)

Most athletic directors are reluctant to open the books, and one administrator explained why specific information on dollars and cents was considered "highly confidential." "If one of our benefactors sees a glowing picture," he said, "he may put his checkbook away and decide, 'They don't need any money.' "

Some skeptics, though, doubt that big-time sports powers are doing as poorly as they sometimes insist.

"I can't believe those big universities that fill stadiums and gymnasiums are losing money," said Bill Bradley, the former All-American basketball star at Princeton. "It's always another story when someone has to open their books and explain certain items."

Yet, despite Bradley's skepticism, there seemed little doubt that the seventies brought a flood of red ink to most of the nation's college sports programs, perhaps to 90 percent of them. Most have begun to economize in little ways: fewer overnight trips, meals in their opponents' dining halls instead of at motels, purchase of equipment months ahead of price increases. Some colleges economize, though, in big ways: no more football, no more freshman or junior varsity teams.

At Slippery Rock in Pennsylvania, which had a sports budget of $100,000 and a deficit of $80,000, efforts were made to generate some television revenue—but they failed. "We're looking for

HITTING THE OLD BOTTOM LINE

Football glory carries a high price tag, and the University of Colorado's athletic budget for fiscal 1972–73 shows why. The budget, published in the *Chronicle of Higher Education*, is as follows:

INCOME

Gate receipts	$1,423,000
Conference share of bowls and TV	297,700
Concessions, parking, etc.	70,600
Student activity fees	140,000
Contributions (development fund)	83,600
Tuition waivers (by legislature)	188,000
Investment income	29,000
Miscellaneous income	10,000
Total	$2,241,900

EXPENSES

Coaching staff salaries	335,600
Office expenses	138,400
Recruiting expenses	70,800
Training table	119,000
Student aid (scholarships)	507,300
Training and medical service	42,300
Game expenses	289,100
Equipment	54,300
Tutoring	6,300
Publicity	16,000
Band	148,900
Repayment to Flatiron Club	43,400
Interest on stadium and payment bonds	78,800
Department salaries (ex. coaches)	163,700
Plant operation	74,900
Capital improvement	175,500
Total	$2,264,300

the good athlete, too," says the athletic director, Dr. Robert E. Raymond. "Our teams are top quality. We almost got into the Rockne Bowl last December. We'd love to have television exposure, but the networks haven't put us on."

Among the private institutions, Harvard and Marquette are

good examples of different kinds of frugality in the running of an athletic department during a period of inflation. Marquette makes money on a somewhat limited program, and regards it as a profit for the 11,000-student university. Harvard loses money on a much broader program but refuses to use the word "deficit," preferring to call it a "legitimate expense in the educational process."

The Marquette budget of "less than $1 million" covers seven intercollegiate sports. Harvard's budget of "less than $3 million" covers men's varsity and freshmen teams in nineteen intercollegiate sports, junior varsity teams, eleven women's sports for Radcliffe, intramural competition for nearly half the college's 5,000 male undergraduates, and an extensive program of recreational sports for members of the entire university family.

Harvard estimates its annual sports revenue at "about $1 million," half of it from football and $50,000 from hockey, its only other money-maker. It employs twenty-three year-round coaches, twenty-one seasonal coaches, eight full-time trainers, six part-time doctors, an administrative staff of thirteen, a full-time operator for the laundry, the equipment repairman, three other equipment men, and twenty-four men for the maintenance of buildings and grounds. In addition, it pays forty-three part-time instructors in the recreational sports that are not on a varsity or other formal level.

"We have a diversified but antiquated athletic plant," says Robert Watson, the athletic director at Harvard. "The priority goes to providing as much total participation as possible."

Watson is quick to point out, almost proudly, that the press box in Harvard Stadium is seventy-one years old and that no Harvard coach (top salary: $25,000) makes as much as a full professor. At some colleges, full professors don't make as much as "full" football coaches.

Marquette dropped varsity football in 1961 because of heavy financial losses. It eliminated freshman and jayvee teams in 1973, when freshmen at all colleges (except in the Ivy League) became eligible for varsity competition. However, its basketball team, coached by Al McGuire, has won twenty or more games for eight straight seasons, thus qualifying for a postseason tournament each time.

The Warriors play sixteen home games a year at the Milwaukee Arena, which seats 10,938, and all of them have been sellouts (at $3 and $4 a ticket) for the last two years. "That generates the revenues, along with radio and television," Prpish says. "The people are behind us now. But a 15-and-10 year, we could feel it at the gate."

If the handwriting was on the wall, it appeared on the wall of Hofstra University on Long Island as the 1974–75 school year began. In a "Memo on Athletics," the president, Robert L. Payton, put it this way:

> "Hofstra University is reshaping its athletic programs to conform to its educational and financial priorities. On recommendation of Robert L. Payton, University President, the Board of Trustees has acted to reduce sharply the heavy subsidies of intercollegiate athletics. Beginning Sept. 1, 1975, the University administration must achieve a reduction of approximately $300,000 from the present level of $475,000, exclusive of financial aid.
>
> "Beyond the financial guidelines, the President announced that recommendations for a wholly new athletic program and philosophy will be submitted in detail to the Board of Trustees within two months, following further consultation with students, faculty, athletic staff, alumni, community leaders and individual trustees.
>
> "As a result of intensive discussions with representatives of all these groups, President Payton reported to the Board that the following general guidelines have emerged:
>
> "(1). Hofstra University will continue to insist that its admission standards and academic performance standards be protected against any erosion.
>
> "(2). There is wide consensus that the University should preserve intercollegiate athletics, and that a viable program can be developed within the new financial limitations.
>
> "(3). The University should try to protect those intercollegiate programs that have played the most important role in the life of the University and that have achieved quality as well as continuing support from students and others. In any case, all

financial commitments to present athletes will be protected as long as they remain at Hofstra.

"(4). The University should expand and strengthen its intramural and recreational athletic programs to ensure suitable opportunities for students interested in intercollegiate sports that may be terminated from lack of support or because of excessive cost.

"(5). Specific suggestions have identified sports which should be maintained at the intercollegiate level: various constituencies strongly support basketball, football, lacrosse and wrestling. Making such choices must be an expression of campus as well as community opinion.

"(6). Complete review of all of our athletic programs for women students will also have to be reviewed and new policies developed.

"(7). In basketball, where Board policy to improve the program was taken in 1970, a new scheduling philosophy would reflect the University's determination to stress competition with other institutions of comparable or higher academic standards. Football would continue within the Metropolitan Conference; schedules in wrestling and lacrosse would also reflect emphasis on competition in the metropolitan area and within the geographical region.

"(8). To insure that there are no discrepancies between the University's stated athletic policies and its practices and standards, the University will call upon qualified external auditors for an annual review of all athletic programs. This annual audit would be conducted by organizations entirely independent of intercollegiate athletics but fully informed about University practices and traditions."

Getting down to the nitty-gritty of this last point, President Payton specified that the annual "audit" would include a complete review of "all admissions of athletes whose names appear on any intercollegiate roster; an audit of the academic records of all continuing athletes, including the actions of the admissions office, committees on admissions and academic standing; an audit of all financial aid received by any athlete participating in University programs." He continued with a real thunderbolt from the mountaintop: "this annual audit will be published and its findings made available *to the press.*"

Without waiting for the gasps from the audience to subside, President Payton moved right along with his *magna carta* of sports-on-campus:

"(9). Reorganization of staff in the athletic department will be based on a nucleus of qualified fulltime coaches, each of whom will be required to carry multiple responsibilities in intramural and recreational programs, in teaching or in administration. No coach would be expected to give fulltime to a single sport, including basketball.

"(10). Around this nucleus of fulltime coaches, the University would continue to draw on the abundance of talented area coaches who can serve only on a part-time basis.

"(11). To defray the costs of the intercollegiate program and to expand and further improve the popular intramural and recreational programs, fund-raising efforts will continue to be conducted among interested alumni and other community leaders."

The impact of those changes, President Payton concluded in a neat understatement, "suggest the direction that a completely revised athletic program might take at Hofstra University." Meanwhile, the "discussions" went on, and those taking part included members of the University Senate and Student Senate, standing committees of the faculty, alumni, community representatives—and members of the athletic staff.

It may have been the best of times or it may have been the worst of times. Or maybe Hofstra was just beating others to the punch. But, whatever the prompting, the college was going to dramatic lengths to answer the question besetting all colleges with sports pressures in the seventies: What price victory?

CHAPTER VIII

TV: All Things
to All People

Economics, a field of learning taught at every college and university in the land, is known for excellent reasons as "the dismal science." Supply and demand. Bad money driving out good money. Full employment. The affluent society. Marginal units, cyclical recession, balance of international payments, the gold standard, managing money, bulls and bears in the stock market, statistical analysis—and lots of red ink.

And on many a campus, not far from the Economics Department, groups of worried men in the Athletic Department grapple with the dismal science of keeping red ink from inundating the green grass of the football stadium. For them, in the 1970s, the leading problem is stark: how to find a supply of money to keep up with the demands of inflation, how to keep halfbacks fed and quarterbacks housed, how to fill grandstands and empty stomachs at the training table. In short, how to pay the bills of the varsity team, which may in turn pay the bills of the Economics Department.

But, as any red-blooded economist will suggest, it never hurts to discover an "outside" source of cash. And, as any red-blooded coach will suggest, there's no sugar daddy like television.

Fortunately for both departments, the decade opened with the sugar daddy in full pursuit of people to project across the TV screens of the country. The search for "talent" that had started with the arrival of television after World War II was still continuing, and the three major networks were still hunting for sports stars as hungrily as the coaches were hunting for them. True, pro football provided the chief lure, just as pro baseball, hockey, and basketball did. But the impact was felt all the way down into the college ranks because: (1) most colleges played their football games on Saturday afternoon, when the pros did not; and (2) most college football stars presumably went through the undergraduate "system" in order to graduate to pro games on Sunday afternoon.

"The prices we pay," said Roone Arledge, president of sports for the American Broadcasting Company, referring to the prices for buying rights to broadcast sports events, "are valid only in relation to each other. Since antitrust laws won't let the networks talk with each other about prices for certain events, we have to go in swinging with the biggest dollar we dare to spend so the competition doesn't cream us. It's absurd, but we're trapped."

"It was like a patriotic cause," said Carl Lindemann, the vice-president of sports programming for the National Broadcasting Company, as he recalled the scramble for rights to games in the early days. "Betrayal meant death."

Everybody agreed that none of the networks could particularly afford to pay the escalating prices for sports, but then none of them could particularly afford *not* to pay them, either. So they all chased after the commissioners of pro sports, and the czars of college sports, offering top dollar in exchange for an exclusive seat in the broadcast booth over the 50-yard line. And, as long as the market held firm, it proved a bonanza for the leagues and teams and universities that had attracted the "winners" into their sports factories.

As the seventies began, the broadcasting people were committing themselves to tabs like these for football alone:

For college and pro games—$62,500,000.
For local radio rights to N.F.L. games—$2,000,000.
For local preseason rights to N.F.L. games—$375,000.
For local radio and delayed-TV rights to 125 college games—
$1,305,375.

Within the skyscraper offices of the networks in Manhattan, the slices of the sports pie were carefully sorted and guarded. It developed, for instance, that NBC-TV had lined up eighty-two American Conference games in the N.F.L. plus the divisional play-offs and the championship game itself (for $15,000,000), the Gator Bowl college game (for $200,000), the Senior Bowl college game (for $50,000), the Orange Bowl game (for $700,000), the Rose Bowl game ($1,400,000), and the Super Bowl game ($2,500,000).

A couple of blocks north, the people at CBS had staked out the National Conference of the pro league (for $20,000,000), the N.F.L. All-Star game ($1,000,000), various playoffs and championships as part of the pro package, and the Sun Bowl college game and Cotton Bowl college romp at undisclosed figures.

Nearby, the boys at ABC-TV were scheduling eleven telecasts and twenty-four regional games for the National Collegiate Athletic Association (for $12,000,000), plus the Coaches All-American game, the College All-Star game, the Liberty Bowl, the North-South Shrine game, the East-West Shrine game, the Sugar Bowl, the Hula Bowl, and a new package of fourteen Monday-night pro games ($8,500,000).

Now, a few years later, the relative value of all these slices of the pie has changed—along with the audience ratings—but the basic rate of exchange was established as the networks, pros, and colleges moved into the seventies. And the radio networks of all three national systems, of course, were making separate deals for many of the same events, on the theory that the radio audience on any given afternoon constituted a different commercial market from the television audience.

As far as the colleges involved in the coverage were concerned, the good news for the pocket-weary alumni and finance
officers broke down into these payoffs from radio and local TV
alone:

Conference	Members	Radio Stations	TV Stations	Total Rights
Atlantic Coast	8	240	13	$73,500
Big Eight	8	228	20	98,500
Big Ten	10	303	27	156,000
Ivy League	8	59	2	13,475
Mid-America	6	22	3	10,600
Missouri Valley	7	21	4	16,000
Pacific Eight	8	131	14	328,400
Southeastern	10	576	42	252,000
Southern	7	36	2	7,500
Western Athletic	8	73	3	39,200
Independents	38	619	83	217,700

Outside of this coast-to-coast spread, some colleges like
Notre Dame stood apart with their own deals for radio rights, as
they usually stood apart on the football field. Notre Dame received
$50,000 from the Mutual network for radio rights to its games,
plus its share of national TV, plus perhaps half a million dollars
for a major bowl appearance, after it revised its policy against such
appearances as the decade moved into its present inflationary
"squeeze" phase.

If these operations represented ripples in the pond of com-
mercialized sports, the ripples became waves as they extended into
the marketplace. In order to get the money they were offering the
professional leagues and colleges, the broadcasting people had to
sell "time" in their game programs; so they headed for the advertising agencies even before the football contracts were signed.

The cost, they reported to the advertisers, would break down
into something like $65,000 for one minute of commercial time—
"a message from our sponsor"—on the N.C.A.A. games. That's
right: $65,000 a minute. Or if a potential sponsor was willing to

buy a whole package of such spots on a series of regular-season games, he would get a sort of wholesale price of only $53,000 a minute. And if the Liberty, Sugar, and Hula Bowls were thrown in, the cost could be beat all the way down to $50,500 a minute.

Professors in the Economics Department could inform quarterbacks in the Athletic Department, of course, that the same sort of money "package" would be available after they turned pro. That is, the lesson was clear: maintain your attractiveness and your success on the gridiron over a long period of time, and cash would continue to flow. If the success resulted in an invitation to appear in a postseason bowl game, then the school might pocket as much as $500,000 more. Elementary economics, Watson.

At the pro level, to cast the lesson into advanced economics, CBS-TV was offering advertisers a selection. The "white" package of goodies contained five Sunday games (the second half of doubleheaders), two Saturday games, and a Thanksgiving Day happening: all for $50,000 a minute. The "blue" package included three preseason combinations at the bargain-basement price of $40,000 a minute. The "red" package, for big spenders, listed fourteen Sunday games, the Eastern and Western pro championships, and the National Conference title game—at $70,000 a minute.

At NBC, the package plan ranged from single games on Saturday or Sunday at $35,000 a minute, preseason games at $40,000, Thanksgiving Day at $65,000, Sunday doubleheaders at $65,000, and the American Conference playoff at $70,000, to the conference title game itself at $110,000 a minute. If anybody had any money left after that, the Rose Bowl game—the banner event of the college season—was available at $120,000 for sixty seconds of message. Beyond that, the Super Bowl came at $200,000 a minute.

What does all this mean to me, a mere college senior? asks the 230-pound lad in the back of the economics class, twirling a football in his right hand during the lecture. Well, the professor might reply, consider the classic case of Joe Willie Namath, who was a senior at the University of Alabama in the days when all this "packaging" of sports events was starting to build up.

Joe Willie at the time was the first among equals in the Class of 1965: equals at firing footballs through the air on Saturday afternoons. His contemporaries included John Huarte at Notre Dame, Craig Morton at the University of California, Archie Roberts at Columbia, and Steve Tensi at Florida State. But many pro scouts, especially those for the New York Jets, were convinced that Namath was the man most likely to succeed in that glittering class of quarterbacks, and Coach Bear Bryant of Alabama, in a rush of pride, called him simply "the best athlete I've ever coached."

When it came to grades—football grades, not academic grades—nobody topped Joe Willie, either. George Sauer, Sr., the chief spy for the Jets, credited him with these marks, based on ratings of 1 down to 5 in football skill: quickness—1; agility—1; strength—2; reaction time—1; coordination—1; size potential—1; durability—2; speed for position—2; intelligence—1; character—2; aggressiveness—1; pride—1. In short, Professor Sauer wrote, "He will be everybody's Number One draft choice."

He was almost right, but not quite. When the pros held their draft sessions—one for the N.F.L. and one for the rival A.F.L.—the New York Giants got first pick in recognition of their record of only two victories the year before. Although they were losing the great Y.A. Tittle at quarterback, they still drafted a running back first: Tucker Frederickson of Auburn. Later in the first round for the National League, the St. Louis Cardinals had their first shot and picked Namath of Alabama.

There was some suspicion that the Cardinals were serving as a stalking-horse for another N.F.L. club, maybe even the Giants. But it was no time for tricks; it was a time for putting up or shutting up. So, when the bidding reached $389,000 for Namath's services, the Cardinals dropped out and left him to the Jets of the A.F.L.

Namath still had one game left to play as a senior in college, the Orange Bowl game on New Year's Day against Texas, and he had to play it on a collapsing right knee. But even before that final fling in college, he and Sonny Werblin of the Jets' high command shook hands on the agreement that guaranteed his future. For a three-year contract, plus a fourth optional year, the Jets promised the twenty-year-old Alabama senior these considerations:

Salary (4 seasons at $25,000 per)	$100,000
Bonus for signing with them	$200,000
"Scouting" jobs for his three brothers and brother-in-law (at $10,000 a year each)	$120,000
Lincoln Continental (green)	$7,000

The package worked out to $427,000 and included some advanced-economics features like a deferred payment on the bonus so that it could be spread out for several years *after* his playing career had ended. With his flank thus secured, so to speak, Namath went out and buckled his knee during a practice session before the Orange Bowl game. However, he put on a pair of sneakers for the main event, completed eighteen of thirty-seven passes for 255 yards and two touchdowns, just missed scoring another on a quarterback sneak at the end, and lost to Texas, 21 to 17.

The Texas undergraduates included some future capitalists, too: Jim Hudson, George Sauer, Jr., Pete Lammons, and John Elliott, all of whom wound up alongside Namath on Werblin's New York Jets. But no member of the Class of 1965—whether majoring in economics *or* football—left the campus that June with a better package than Joe Willie Namath of Beaver Falls, Pennsylvania.

Five years later, a senior at the University of Southern California with the intriguing name of O. J. Simpson reflected on *his* lesson in economics. He had played thirty games for Southern Cal and had graduated as the most celebrated running back in the school's history. Then he was drafted by the Buffalo Bills, one of the twenty-six teams in the newly merged pro football leagues.

That meant he could negotiate only with the Bills and would not have the choice that Namath had enjoyed at Alabama in the days before the leagues merged—and thereby eliminated one of the most profitable auction markets anywhere for college athletes.

Simpson wasn't troubled much by the prospect of settling on a money figure with Buffalo, because even without an auction for his services he knew that the contract would make him a millionaire. But he was troubled somewhat by the thought of starting his pro career 3,000 miles from home in a city that was often snowbound, and for a team that had achieved the worst record in pro ball the season before by winning only one of fourteen games.

But O.J. had a few things going for him—a few things that the other members of Southern Cal's graduating class did not have going for them. He was the Number One draft choice in pro football, and that made him automatically the country's most expensive senior. His agent was Chuck Barnes, a talent specialist for Sports Headliners—and for the chemistry majors in the audience, an agent is someone who runs up the price for an undergraduate who did not spend his afternoons in a chemistry lab when the football coach wanted him to run for the varsity.

Barnes wasted no time making his pitch on Simpson's behalf: $650,000 for five years of running with a football. That would include an annual salary of $100,000 and a bonus of $150,000. The owner of the Buffalo club, Ralph Wilson, offered $50,000 a season for a total of $250,000. They were $400,000 apart.

Somehow, though, they bridged the gap, leaving Wilson with the most prized football player on the campus scene and with the problem of paying his salary. One way or another, however, it would all work out—Simpson might fill the stadium at $8 a seat, and the sugar daddy in the television booth might supply the rest. Then the television people would head for the ad agencies to sell the commercials to make up the money they had paid Ralph Wilson and his colleagues to bring O. J. Simpson into the wonderful world of professional sports.

To lighten the mood with some badinage at the critical mo-

(*The New York Times*)

Sports spectacular: In the supercharged atmosphere of national television, the Purdue marching band serenades Ohio State with 310 musicians and 20 majorettes. As in show biz, somebody must pay the
bills: frequently TV.

ment in the negotiations, Simpson told Wilson that he had had a bad dream after his senior season at Southern Cal. "It was a nightmare," he joked. "I dreamed I was drafted by the Buffalo Bills."

Wilson, remembering the half-dozen quarterbacks who had been injured on his payroll the year before and recoiling at the size of the talent package he was underwriting, replied: "I had a nightmare, too. I dreamed you were a flop."

As things turned out, neither O. J. Simpson nor Joe Namath disappointed classmates or new employers. The problem, outside of staying healthy, was staying solvent at a time when costs for everything were rising out of sight and threatening to curtail the entire system—from shoulder pads for the freshman team to bonus contracts for veteran pros. Everything costs somebody something, and no exceptions are made for sports heroes and their tools. The 360,000 baseballs used in the big leagues each season cost about $2 apiece. And when it comes to footballs, at $26 each, teams like the Los Angeles Rams use 250 a season, while the Chicago Bears for some reason eat up 400 a year. The Bears pay $35 for a game jersey, $38 for a helmet, $33 for game pants, $50 for a heavy warm-up jersey shirt, $50 for a sideline cape, $40 to $50 for a pair of shoulder pads, $15 for hip pads. And maybe $600,000 for a college running back.

To recoup one's investment, whether at the college level or in the pros, the idea is to develop a "show" that will sell, whether it is 80,000 seats in Ohio State's stadium on Saturday afternoon or 10,000,000 living rooms with TV sets on Sunday afternoon. Either way, the show's the thing. When Bobby Riggs hustled Margaret Court into their famous tennis match in 1974, the TV rights were grabbed by CBS for only $45,000. But when Riggs pushed his advantage into a "Battle of the Sexes" match against Billie Jean King, it became a national circus that cost ABC a cool $750,000 for the TV rights.

The college bowl games in recent years have also led to some crucial bidding behind the campus scenes. For example, ABC, which had an arrangement with the Sugar Bowl, found that it was threatened by competing attractions: NBC's Orange Bowl game and CBS's Cotton Bowl game. So it altered its contract, kicked in $60,000 extra, and invited the two top college teams in the country to play in the 1974 Sugar Bowl: Notre Dame and Alabama.

Roone Arledge denied that ABC had used pressure tactics to land both colleges. But he acknowledged that the network, which televises college games on Saturdays throughout the season, had impressed both colleges with the notion that "we think you owe it to us and the Sugar Bowl."

On the same day that Notre Dame edged Alabama in their memorable game in the Sugar Bowl, Ohio State was playing Southern Cal in the Rose Bowl—with Arledge's cameras recording it all. Back in the midlands, the University of Michigan was somewhat disappointed that its undefeated football team hadn't been picked to represent the Big Ten in the game. But Michigan still had enough grasp of the economic realities to be happy that Big Ten champions always have a Rose Bowl to attend on New Year's Day.

"We and the rest of the conference schools that won't be there," conceded Don Canham, the athletic director at Ann Arbor, "will get more than $100,000 each as our share. Without that money and a good football season, our budget would be in the red."

Now, though, amateurs and pros alike are feeling the pinch of inflated costs. So more pressure has been applied all along the line: recruiting has become more selective and perhaps more critical, winning has become more urgent, and the bottom line has become a matter of life and death to many college sports programs.

Some colleges have tried to hold off doomsday by raising the price of a seat to a football game. The Southeastern Conference went from $6 a seat to $7, and is considering $8. But that is getting dangerously close to the price of a ticket to a pro game. Others have looked to television to increase the ante, and ABC-TV has obliged by raising its contribution for "exclusive" rights to

N.C.A.A. games from $13,500,000 for two seasons to $15,-900,000. Still other colleges have turned to their professional neighbors for help: the University of Illinois signed the Chicago Bears and St. Louis Cardinals to play exhibition games in its stadium at Champaign and expects to collect $100,000 or more for each game.

Cost cutting also has been cranked into the equation by the colleges. The N.C.A.A. voted to restrict the number of football scholarships that a member school could give in one year to thirty, with the total not to exceed 105 in four years. Before the "restriction," which might make some economics departments gasp in envy, some colleges gave as many as 140 football grants. Another cost-cutting move was the decision to allow freshmen to compete in major varsity sports, thereby eliminating some freshman and junior varsity teams.

At the University of Minnesota, though, the red ink keeps flowing despite recent efforts to economize. In five years, the university has accumulated deficits of $500,000 in its varsity sports programs; Paul Giel, the athletic director, says the total will hit $800,000 in the next three years, and adds:

"We've tried to economize, but we can't possibly do that enough. If the school wants to continue having a well-rounded sports program, it'll have to find ways to fund it like any other department on campus."

"The days when athletic departments were flush with money are gone for good," lamented J.D. Morgan, athletic director at U.C.L.A., a college with far better luck and far more prosperity in sports than most. "We've had fine teams lately, but we're not that far ahead. Something has to give somewhere."

Still, despite the decision by more and more colleges to give up big-time sports, the lure remains: sports programs can pay university bills as well as incur university bills. So the talent search goes on, in spite of the revised rules.

At Kent State University in Ohio, the sports budget totals $1,100,000 and the sports deficit totals $955,000. But the president of the university, Glenn A. Olds, an eager fan and a onetime professional boxer, has refused to panic.

"All our efforts," he told Richard Starnes, who was research-ing the problem for the *Chronicle of Higher Education*, "should be bent to put the principal emphasis on the educational program, but I consider intercollegiate athletics as a prime illustration of an educational program. I don't take the view that intercollegiate ath-letics is a public relations gimmick for the purpose of refurbishing the public image of the university.

"I recognize that it represents the flowering of excellence like all scales of competence, whether music, speech or drama, or the special talent of a particular segment of the university. I have argued, therefore, that it should be measured like all our co-curric-ular activities, not as an addendum but as a critical complement and enrichment of the educational program.

"I've argued that so long as we remain competitive in these areas of excellence, we should be certain that any efforts in reduc-tion of support be done conference-wide. In short, I am a poor loser, and I think it would be ill-advised to reduce the support of our program unilaterally—independent of, or unrelated to, any other teams. I favor reduction of costs, but it should be done uniformly throughout the conference."

He meant the Mid-America Conference, which does not send its championship teams to the Rose Bowl the way the Big Ten does. But the conference champion last year, Kent State, did go to the Tangerine Bowl and, even at that level of operating, the college and the conference found the situation growing sticky.

"Excesses hurt everybody, just as success helps everybody," President Olds went on. "I don't object to big-time teams getting on national television. It's good for sports generally.

"If we were to fill all the seats in the new stadium each Saturday that we play football, and everyone would pay the full price, we would be taking in $100,000 every Saturday afternoon."

Until the stadium is filled every Saturday afternoon, though, it seems likely that Ohio's taxpayers will be picking up the tab for

Kent State's losses in sports, as television or alumni or tuition payments are doing on other campuses. As President Olds was speaking, his new stadium stood nearby with 30,000 seats and a $4,000,000 price tag. It was estimated that about $81 of the annual tuition and fees paid by each of Kent State's 20,000 students went to pay off the bonded debt on the stadium, its parking lot, an ice arena, and a new student union.

Mr. Olds concedes that the stadium is used only five or six times a year. And he also concedes that, brave outlook or not, the students or their parents will be paying off the bond issue for the next forty years.

CHAPTER IX

... And $15
for Laundry

"In the event such aid exceeds commonly accepted educational expenses (i.e., tuition and fees; room and board; required course-related supplies and books, and incidental expenses not in excess of fifteen dollars per month) during the undergraduate career of the recipient, it shall be considered 'pay' for participation in intercollegiate athletics."

Article Three, *Constitution and Interpretations* of the National Collegiate Athletic Association.

The "tips" arrive in the nice new headquarters building in Shawnee Mission, Kansas, by letter, telephone, telegram, and newspaper clipping. Usually they report or suggest that a college coach is attempting to strengthen his team by going outside the rules of the National Collegiate Athletic Association and the 664 colleges that pursue sports under its administrative umbrella. Sometimes the tips and complaints trickle in; sometimes they pour in. However they arrive, they are checked out by a onetime college athlete and his "staff" of three recruiting bloodhounds plus the six others who joined them early in 1975.

The onetime athlete is Warren Scott Brown, the thirty-five-year-old assistant executive director of the N.C.A.A. He is in charge of investigations. And because he commands a tiny staff with a mountain of violations to study from the Atlantic to the Pacific to the Hawaiian Islands, he has learned to be as inventive as some of the 664 colleges that he investigates.

Brown and his staff are armed with a healthy suspicion that money corrupts, with a limited budget, with an impossible work load, with charge and counter-charge, and with a 4,500-word set of rules that forms the nucleus of the Bible of pure amateurism for the nation's colleges and universities. The key passages are grouped under Article Three of the N.C.A.A.'s *Constitution and Interpretations*, with the heading "Principles for the Conduct of Intercollegiate Athletics."

Section 1 stakes out the guiding principle: "An amateur student-athlete is one who engages in athletics for the educational, physical, mental and social benefits he derives therefrom and to whom athletics is an avocation." So far, so good. Then, coming to grips with the definition of such an amateur student-athlete, the section declares:

"A student-athlete shall not be eligible for intercollegiate athletics if (1) he takes or has taken pay, or has accepted the promise of pay, in any form, for participation in athletics, or (2) he has entered into an agreement of any kind to compete in professional athletics, or to negotiate a professional contract, or (3) he has directly or indirectly used his athletic skill for pay in any form; however, a student-athlete may accept scholarships or educational grants-in-aid from his institution which do not conflict with the governing legislation of this Association."

That is, which do not go beyond tuition, room, board, books, and $15 a month for incidental expenses—the latter commonly, and sometimes jocularly, referred to as "laundry money." Which is where Warren Brown and his army of three investigators get into the act.

Cheating, Brown seems to feel, is no worse than it used to be,

(*Associated Press*)
Members of the N.C.A.A.
are allowed to pay an
athlete his tuition, room,
board, books, and $15 a
month for laundry and
incidentals. To make sure
that they pay no more,
Warren Brown and a tiny
staff of "supersleuths"
patrol 664 colleges
searching for violations.

which is another way of saying it's no better than it used to be. But whatever the level of cheating, he attacks it with one arm tied behind his back: neither he nor his staff enjoys subpoena powers or any of the enforcement weapons usually enjoyed by the good guys chasing after the bad guys. "If somebody at a college tells us to just get the heck out of here," he says, "then we get out."

"We find out things, though," he notes. "We can get somebody who has left a school to tell us about violations. Get a coach fired and he'll talk. And sometimes you run into people who just can't lie."

Sometimes the violators leave a record, or a "trail." Brown remembers the celebrated case of Long Beach State, which was given its severe probation penalty because of violations that included expensive gifts for athletes.

"Those were major things," he recalls. "There were bank notes. You've got to have somebody get those for you. You just can't walk in off the street and say, 'Show me a copy of your bank notes.' And then, apartments were paid for. You've got to have people willing to tell you about that. It's not an impossible task, but it's a roadblock that you have to face every once in a while."

Given his traditional background and the fact that he was a scholarship athlete himself, Brown's zeal astounds many of the people he encounters in the course of his investigations, especially the people he is investigating.

He was probably one of the few athletes ever recruited out of Lee's Summit, Missouri, where he was born in 1940. The town isn't far from Kansas City. He grew into a tall, slender, and agile teen-ager who played high-school basketball well enough to draw recruiters from Kansas State, Kansas, and Missouri, and to receive offers also from Drake, William Jewell College, and Central Missouri State.

"I chose Kansas State because they just came off a great year," he explains. "They had Bob Boozer and they had beaten the Kansas team that had Wilt Chamberlain. Secondly, I liked the coach, Tex Winter. And number three, my grandmother hated Kansas University."

As a student, he concedes, he was "pretty damned usual." Usual, that is, for a varsity athlete. "I was in on all the campus activities with the 'in' group, so to speak."

But in his position as a big man on campus, he "never heard" of recruiting violations, "and I think I would have." When he graduated, with a degree in physical education, he had a high scholastic ranking plus three seasons of varsity basketball that included one Big Eight title. He went on to Indiana University to get his master's degree in physical education, and then went into the Air Force for three years.

When he was hired by the N.C.A.A. in 1966, only one man was investigating athletic irregularities—Art Bergstrom, who had been saddled with the lonely position for years. By 1970, Brown was in charge of a three-man staff: that is, the original police force of two had doubled. Each member of his "force" also was a former varsity athlete: Lynn Nance, once an agent for the Federal

Bureau of Investigation, who had played basketball at Washington; Bill Hunt, a graduate of the Southern Methodist Law School, who had played tennis for Texas Christian before that; and Dave Berst, who had played baseball and basketball at MacMurray.

Over the years, each of the many rules has become ingrained in Brown's consciousness. Now, says a colleague, "Warren's the only guy in the world who can give you interpretations off the top of his head of every rule in that big book." Still, the tall, calm-mannered Brown replies, when asked a specific question: "Just a moment. Let me look up the record."

One athletic director of a penalized college admitted that he had been impressed by Brown's thoroughness. He recalled that his president wasn't even aware of what had been going on when he was pleading his college's case before the N.C.A.A.'s committee on infractions.

"But that was before Brown's evidence came up," the athletic director said, "and then, item by item, step by step, Brown proved his case. I thought the prexy's chin would fall through the floor. He never knew what was going on. But Brown did—and we were nailed. And Warren never blinked an eye."

However, despite successes like that one, Brown and his small band of sleuths usually find themselves in the predicament of a man fighting a forest fire with a garden hose. The colleges have become so trapped in the recruiting system that they now insist they cannot escape because it is a "necessary evil," though they stand to lose national ranking, post-season bowl money, and television income if they cheat.

"The pressure to win is a hell of a lot more than just hiring and firing a coach," says Don Canham, athletic director at the University of Michigan. "It's keeping your whole program going. Recruiting is a justified pursuit, without question. Let me put it another way: It's a necessary evil. For instance, if we did not recruit and have great football teams [at Michigan], we wouldn't have anything going. We wouldn't have any money. It's absolutely essential in our system in amateur athletics today."

Essential or not, amateur or not, Warren Brown and his enforcers continue to see unmistakable signs that the system inevi-
tably snowballs, and they also see their inquiries leading to public
penalties against member colleges on the average of more than
once a month. Even so, many educators and athletic officials believe this is only a fraction of the total number of colleges actually
recruiting improperly. Some of the members believe this, too. The
University of Texas even called for all members of the N.C.A.A.
to contribute funds to beef up the enforcement procedures, and
volunteered $5,000 to start things rolling toward "increasing ef-
forts in enforcement, particularly in recruiting."

Some officials, like the Rev. Edmund P. Joyce, executive vice-
president of Notre Dame, said they would contribute to such a
fund. But the other colleges in the association nevertheless voted
against appropriations to add to Brown's staff—although they had
previously approved the construction of the new N.C.A.A. headquarters building in Shawnee Mission at a cost of more than $1.5
million.

"The record shows people are cheating in athletics just as
they are in other walks of life," says Brown. "It's not, in my
opinion, getting any better because we have people out finding stuff
every day, and four times a year our infractions committee pen-
alizes four or five schools. That's twenty schools a year. So people
are doing it."

The violations, when they are detected, often seem flagrant.
Automobiles have been purchased for athletes and money has been
supplied beyond the $15 for laundry, and beyond the scholarship
aid that sometimes amounts to $5,000 a year alone.

"They just don't go out and give automobiles," Brown says.
"They backstop themselves some way. We've had instances where,
on the bank records of loan papers, it's the young man or his
parents—but we've proved that they got the cash to make the
payments. That's the same as giving him a car. They get a car in
their own name and somebody else makes the payments.

"Kids also get cash to go home. Several hundred dollars to

buy airline tickets. Or they get money to pay for their apartment each month while they're in school—$200 or such for 10 months."

Since athletes have been offered inducements by colleges for nearly a century, why hasn't any significant progress been made in eliminating the practice?

"The recruited athlete today isn't protecting the coach's job," replies Canham of Michigan. "He's supporting the whole ball of wax. Recruiting is worse now than it used to be because it's not just the coach's job; it's the whole damn program that's going to go down the drain. So there's more pressure on the guy to con the kid than ever before. Now if he doesn't win, the whole thing collapses, as it has at some schools.

"The coach himself is getting instructions from up on top. 'You got to get that kid because we got to fill the basketball arena.' They're getting instructions, in some cases, from the college presidents. It's wrong, but how are you going to change it? The system of intercollegiate athletics is not going to change. The only way it's going to change is to collapse. Then, a super conference will be formed out of the wreckage.

"I certainly think there are several schools in the Big Ten and several in the Big Eight and some in the Pacific Coast Conference that cannot go on with it at all. Hell, I think it's impossible for the Big Ten to survive the way it is."

He meant the big Big Ten, one of the country's most important conferences in all sports. It has some of the biggest stadiums, plus such trappings of success in sports as Game of the Week coverage on national television and frequent bowl appearances. Besides Michigan, the conference includes Ohio State, Northwestern, Illinois, Iowa, Indiana, Wisconsin, Minnesota, Michigan State, and Purdue.

For years, the N.C.A.A. depended on one college's "blowing the whistle" on another in order to catch the culprits. This is still a prime source of information for Brown's enforcers, though they rely on many other bits of information. Until the time comes when a better system of "tips" is developed, many colleges insist, the coaches themselves should be more outspoken about violations. "I would tell our coaches, don't complain to me about it," Father Joyce says. "If you know of anything dishonest happening, we should make an issue of it and make it publicly. I think you coaches should all stand up and be counted on something like this."

Paul Dietzel, athletic director and football coach at the University of South Carolina: "I think cheating will destroy athletics. We are not going to cheat, and I'll assure you of one thing—If we're not going to cheat, nobody else is going to cheat against us. And if they do, I am going to turn in their butts, and I make no bones about it. I'm going to turn them in. Now, a lot of people say, we don't want to be a fink, a guy who turns people in. I kind of feel that people who don't want to turn them in are afraid that they might be caught at something they've done."

Bob James, commissioner of the Atlantic Coast Conference and chairman of the N.C.A.A.'s special committee on recruiting, suggests that, when a boy agrees to go to an institution on an athletic scholarship, he be required to sign a notarized statement listing just what the college offered him. This statement should, of course, include only the scholarship and other items permitted by the N.C.A.A. regulations—ideally speaking.

"I think it's equally important," James adds, "that the boy and his parents also list the institutions that offered him aid in excess of the above. Tell us who did offer him more than is allowable."

James also favors a limit on the number of colleges a high-school athlete may visit at the colleges' expense, as well as a limit on the number of times recruiters from one college may visit an athlete at his home. There is no limit on the number of times a coach can talk to a recruit away from the campus, and the travel involved in chasing the boy is one of the most expensive items of all.

"In the area of a heavily recruited athlete," James says, "he'll tell you there are times he doesn't even bother going to his own home. He just wants one night of peace. So he'll go stay with a

"A lot of kids are spoiled because of this system," says Digger Phelps, basketball coach at Notre Dame and one of the younger officials working within the college sports system.

friend. But that doesn't stop the recruiter from spending the evening with his parents.

"Wherever the boy goes, he is sought out. The recruiter is in town for one reason: to seek out this boy. That's his job. If they could be there only two or three times, there would be a considerable reduction in the intrusion on the boy's life."

Richard (Digger) Phelps, the basketball coach at Notre Dame, was successfully recruiting at Fordham before he switched to South Bend. He is younger than many coaches, and that's clearly one of the secrets of his rapport with teen-age athletes.

"A lot of kids are spoiled because of this system," Phelps says. "When you see 100 schools come in to recruit a boy and 90 schools tell him one thing and 10 tell him another thing, a lot of schools are going to confuse the youngster. Believe me, there are a lot of great salesmen in college basketball. It's confusing to the family. It's confusing to the youngster."

To prevent continuous pressure on a boy in his own home, Phelps suggests going farther than James, who would limit the visits. "If you put yourself in a position where there was no off-campus recruiting," Phelps proposes, "that would really shake up a lot of people. I think what is happening in the off-season in basketball is really getting out of hand now. It's costing the colleges money."

Phelps would like to see recruiting curtailed by setting a deadline of May 15, at which time a student should make his final decision on a college.

"Throw it right back at the youngster and the family," he says. "End it. It's ridiculous. Last year we were recruiting in the middle of June. I don't blame the kids. I blame the system. The families don't understand this. They don't go through it every year like we do. It's just once in their family. I've seen families change. From the time you start recruiting them in the fall, they think it's fun. All the coaches coming to town and all that. Believe me, by the last week in April, they can't talk to each other. That's how confused they are. That's how uptight they are. I think we've created a monster."

One major college football coach complains of an even worse intrusion on a boy's time: coaches induce high-school teachers and principals to take a boy out of class in order to speak with a recruiter.

"This should never be allowed," he believes. "A boy should never be taken from a class for this purpose. How can we say we attempt to educate student-athletes if we have such light regard for their high-school class time?"

Yet, as in other areas of the campus life, not everybody agrees with the critics. Dr. John T. Caldwell, Chancellor of North Carolina State University, offers a defense of the college sports programs generally:

"I think the recruiting of athletes has become a part and an almost essential part of the picture of competitive intercollegiate athletics. And I have to justify intercollegiate athletics in the modern vein when I justify recruiting. I, as a matter of fact, wish that we did not have high-pressure recruiting.

"Does it distort the values of these young men? Well, maybe sometimes, yes. But if it distorts them in the direction to think that athletics is all-important, that would be bad. I don't think it works out that way. I think the young men themselves, when they get these grants-in-aid, choose an institution that has an educational program that they want. Eight out of ten of them will do that.

"I frankly would like to think that institutions of a given academic calibre could compete with each other on equal terms without the money factor being a part of it. This is something we haven't found a way to accomplish. This is where I think a lot of the concentrated efforts of the responsible policy-makers in inter-collegiate athletics must be exerted."

Most coaches might applaud the chancellor's high hopes for a controlled and reasoned approach to college sports, but many of them still feel that the temptations will prove too strong along the way. Pete Newell, who was a highly successful basketball coach at San Francisco, Michigan State, and California, went on to become a highly successful executive in the pros, as general manager of the Los Angeles Lakers. To him, looking at it from both sides of the fence, it is a "hell of an indictment of college athletics if, as some people say, you can't get to the top without cheating.

"I know everyone doesn't cheat," Newell says, "but I also know that the prevailing thought is that 'if he can do it, why can't I?' It's become a vicious circle and, in my opinion, it's a bloody shame we are where we are at this moment. I think it's about time for everyone to get in the same boat."

Gary Colson, the basketball coach at little Pepperdine College in California, cherishes no illusions about the price you pay for success: "If our team was on the Top Ten today, we'd have to cheat to get there."

Ralph Miller of Oregon State, also cherishing no illusions, feels the problem is at a peak now: "I guess I'm from the old school, but this kind of thing has no place in intercollegiate athletics. The rules we have, for the most part, are reasonable, and I think we can accept them. Unfortunately, there are men in our profession who feel they have to get around the rules to recruit. These people have given us a black eye. There is still a certain form of greed that makes someone want to cut corners. Will Rogers said something like, 'Graft isn't graft unless you're not getting any.'

"I know several families who would allow their offspring more than usual, but if I had a son who was being recruited and I heard of him getting something illegal, I'd personally escort the coach out of our home. I've taken a lot of pride in my own thing that I've never done this. When I retire, I can look back and say I've never offered a kid anything."

One coach who could not make that statement—one of the many coaches who could not make that statement—is Wayne Vandenburg, who in six years as the head track and field coach at the University of Texas at El Paso earned the reputation as "the fastest mouth in the West." He left the rat race in 1972 to enter private business after a dispute with the athletic department over some of his more imaginative practices, such as using the telephone to recruit a world-class discus thrower from South Africa.

Now, Vandenburg is neither bitter nor embarrassed over his style of recruiting, which shot El Paso into the front ranks in a hurry. Looking back on it all—and after having once described recruiting as "the easiest thing I've ever done"—he concedes: "It's a dirty, dirty business. Some coaches will go to any extreme to get a kid."

Once he stayed three days in Saugus, California (pop. 7,762), to convince the parents of a top prospect, Fred DeBernardi, that El Paso was the right place for their son—in fact, the only place.

"I had tried everything else," he remembers. "So I went out there and told them, 'I'm not leaving until you say Freddie's coming with me.' "

DeBernardi, a muscular shot-putter and discus thrower, enrolled at the college the following semester on a four-year athletic scholarship and went the route: he became a world-class competitor.

"I was after a hurdler from California," Vandenburg recalls, dredging up past battles. "He didn't have the grades to qualify for El Paso, but I was going to see to it that he got grades to qualify. I was going to get him a correspondence course and get him enrolled for a course that he could finish. I had all the lessons. You know, that kind of thing is going on all over the country."

Before Vandenburg could enroll the hurdler in the correspondence course, though, the athlete showed up at a college in the Pacific Eight Conference, which supposedly had higher entrance requirements than El Paso did. So why didn't he protest to the N.C.A.A. and turn in the rival school for recruiting violations?

"I wasn't a sore loser," he says. "I wanted to beat them on the track. I didn't have to turn them in because they had snookered me. That wasn't my style. Besides, I would have probably done the same thing."

Vandenburg used to let little stand in the way of recruiting an athlete, so he wasn't simply talking big when he said "I would have probably done the same thing." He once wrote a series of letters to a British labor union that finally convinced it to let John Bednarski, an apprentice locomotive repairman and a fine distance runner, attend college in the United States—without losing his trade credentials. El Paso, naturally.

Another time, he swayed Steve Williams from the Bronx to El Paso, where he became one of the world's great sprinters, and even recruited several basketball stars who helped the college maintain its national prominence. Once he had athletes on his roster from seven countries, including Australia, Sweden, and Jamaica. His track teams regularly finished among the first three or four at the annual N.C.A.A. meets.

The methods he used in building a national power—at a college previously known, or unknown, as Texas Western—combined an aggressive sales pitch with an astute exploiting of the legal loopholes in the rules. He pushed his methods so well that he enticed prospects away from major track colleges like U.C.L.A., Brigham Young, and Villanova. One incentive, he concedes, was that El Paso's modest entrance requirements allowed some students to be admitted "provisionally," even while they could not qualify for athletic scholarships.

"The athlete might not have been eligible for a grant-in-aid the first year," he remembers, describing a policy that was applicable to all Texas colleges. "But at least you could get him into school, which was an advantage for us and a positive point for the athlete."

Various Federal and state equal-opportunity funds, minority-student scholarships, and work-study grants—all became programs investigated, and tapped, by the thinking man's coach. "I couldn't give a kid an athletic scholarship," he says, "if he didn't qualify under the 1.6 rule [on academic standing]. But if he could qualify for a job and he did all the work, he could fill out the papers."

In recruiting his athletes, Vandenburg became as much a financial adviser as a coach. He checked out every aid program that was available—even Good Neighbor Scholarships for South American students.

When he began working at El Paso, he had twelve full scholarships that covered the allowable basics of tuition, room, board, books, and the legendary $15 a month. But he aggressively went out and acquired equal-opportunity funds for prospects whose family incomes were under $6,000 a year, uncovered work-study grants and summer jobs, and wound up getting financial help for forty-five track athletes at one time. All legally, he insists.

"You legally can't tell a kid that you can get him a job," he notes, turning to another problem zone. "But you always do. You say by the letter of the law, 'I will assist you in trying to help you find proper employment.'"

Most work-study programs at colleges involve campus employment, which Vandenburg says often amount to no work if the athlete is assigned to the athletic department under the coach's supervision. At El Paso, for example, a half-miler named Fernando de la Cerda helped pay the bills for his wife and child by turning the water on and off every night on the football field after practice. For $1.60 an hour.

"Athletes are not supposed to have an advantage over non-athletes," Vandenburg concedes. "But if you don't think that financial-aid officers listen to coaches . . . And financial-aid officers are probably ex-jocks. I don't think any financial-aid officer ever did anything illegal, but I know he wanted us to have a good track team and good football team, so I don't think he ever refused."

Another loophole that he was able to sell as a recruiting device was the opportunity for an athlete to return home as part of a sports trip, say an indoor track meet. It was a device that he saw being used by many other schools especially in chasing prospects from the New York area, which could be easily visited during the indoor-track season.

He also recruited on "the negative side," particularly with black athletes who often had little knowledge of El Paso or the Southwest:

"I told them there were very few black chicks in El Paso, and that they were far away from home. I told them I didn't care if they went out with white chicks, that they could go out with anybody they wanted. But if they were used to being in a situation where you had a lot of black chicks, it wasn't like being in the big city."

For all his brash salesmanship, which often intimidated and irritated his colleagues, Vandenburg strongly denies that he ever sold sex; but he insists sex was used as a weapon against his college:

"Coaches were always saying, 'Yeah, I'll bet they've got the advantage at El Paso; they can take black guys over to Juarez and . . .' "

To Vandenburg, that was negative thinking "because what you're doing is downgrading the kid's ability as a human."

In assessing his own role as a recruiter, Vandenburg admits that his attitude often was too subjective and that, like many coaches, he put too much pressure on himself because of his determination to succeed.

"I always thought I was the savior," he says, referring to cases where he "gambled" in recruiting players who might have had academic or personal problems. And, looking back on his life in the pit of college sports, he acknowledges that maybe he was wrong in "trying to make a judgment in their behalf" and in telling them that his school was the best place for them.

"Nobody has the right to say that," he reasons now. "That's something a young man has to decide for himself."

CHAPTER X

Hold Down
the Booing, Please

WHERE THE PEOPLE ARE IN NEBRASKA

Omaha	347,328
Lincoln	149,518
Memorial Stadium (*on*	
a football Saturday)	76,000
Grand Island	32,358
Hastings	23,580

(SOURCES: *Bureau of the Census University of Nebraska*)

Out there in the frontline trenches of academia, out where the ivory towers rise tall over the green malls and quadrangles, where college means Advanced Biology to some students and Contemporary Lit to others—out there, not everybody is giving it the old "sis-boom-bah" as the rage to win has crept over America's campuses. The library doesn't draw as well as the stadium, that is true enough; the History Department isn't budgeted as handsomely as the Athletic Department, also true; and some of the best faculty brains aren't rewarded in power, prestige, or cash on the same level as the football coach, too true.

But out there, the natives are showing extreme signs of restlessness as the chosen few on the varsity continue hell-bent on their razzle-dazzle careers. They are not the same students who tore things up in the sixties, the decade of activism and of protest against the war in Vietnam. But they still approach the campus scene with the same skeptical eye. And though the old stadiums are still being filled on Saturdays, and though the recruiters are still recruiting and the coaches are still coaching, a lot of the nonvarsity students are no longer cheering. Not at $6,000 a year for book learning.

After sampling campus attitudes toward sports in all types of colleges, from small ones in Maine to large ones in California, *The New York Times* released its results in 1974, a time when athletic programs were coming under their heaviest fire in perhaps half a century. The attitudes of the coaches and athletes were firmly established: we want to "win at any cost," but we "live by the rules," a combination which some observers felt would be a neat trick to reconcile. But the attitudes of the student bodies were less certain. They ranged from old-fashioned "college spirit" all the way to scorn for the way of life that college spirit seemed to suggest. The preponderant feeling among the students was that runaway college spirit—at least as it was related to the gridiron and the basketball court—"went out with Eisenhower, Edsels, and Elvis Presley."

School spirit, for the most part, has apparently gone the way of the student activism that overwhelmed it in the late sixties. Many students expressed a disdain for the bigness of the college sports programs, which they felt ignored the needs of the average undergraduate. Others complained that women's sports programs at many colleges were still being financed as clubs. Still others protested that intramural sports were being lost in the shuffle.

Take the University of Wisconsin, where hockey is king. The college is a member of the Big Ten athletic conference, and, though the football team has been rather silent in recent years, it does try to tackle powerhouses like Ohio State and Michigan. In basketball, the same struggle. But get the Badgers on ice, and they go big-time.

Wisconsin plays about twenty home games a season in the

(*The New York Times/University of Nebraska*)
Third largest city in Nebraska—that's what Memorial Stadium at Lincoln becomes on Saturday afternoons when the Cornhuskers play football at home, as they are doing here against North Carolina State before
76,000 persons.

Dane County Memorial Coliseum, mostly before sellout crowds of 9,000. So the Badgers skate to success both on the ice and at the box office—grossing about $720,000. But they are not always loved.

"I don't pay attention to sports at all," said Harriet Gethertz, a sophomore. "I'm not a big sports freak. I don't like the whole atmosphere, and I don't like the person who follows organized sports."

But Miss Gethertz insisted that it wasn't just sports she disliked; it was "bigness" that turned her off.

"I don't really see the necessity of having a big sports program like the Big Ten," she said. "I'd be satisfied with intramurals. I like to see college as an academic-cultural marketplace, and I don't see any place there for big sports. I'm not against physical fitness; but there's a kind of mindlessness in big sports. I'm more into individual sports like bicycling. I just don't dig the glorification."

At the University of Nebraska, some of the scholars were turned off by bigness, too. On several Saturdays each autumn, 76,000 lovers of Cornhusker football jam Memorial Stadium—many of them students dressed in the school's bright red colors, and all of them in love with the team that in the last ten years has been national champion twice and Big Eight conference champion eight times.

But not all of the 22,000 students on campus worship success of these dimensions. To many, football has become big—big business. And others said they simply didn't "care" for the other sports on the program.

"Football is just too big," said Tim O'Shea, a senior majoring in engineering. "You know something is amiss when the stadium is the third largest city in the state on a home-game day."

It is on a "home-game day" that Grand Island drops to Number Four in the state, behind Omaha, Lincoln—and Memorial Stadium.

Disaffection, though, takes different forms. For some students, big football means overcrowded taverns and parking lots on game days. For others, it means an invasion that they cannot relate to anything that happens the rest of the week, or the rest of the year.

Still, football commands the attention of the undergraduates at Nebraska, despite the problems it brings. "Nothing personal" against it. But the tolerance for football is still not matched in other sports, which many students consider step-children of the "main event" that fills the stadium with red jackets and green money.

Recruiting, moreover, is an unknown to many of the non-athletes at Nebraska. The college spends $150,000 a year on recruiting, about $125,000 of that on football. But few students surveyed on campus had any idea what the figures were. Only one student felt that the recruiters should be watched more closely.

At Wisconsin, the same sort of vagueness about the eternal chase was shown. Bill Foster, a junior, put it this way: "All I know about recruiting is what I've read in several scandal articles. I really don't know, but maybe there shouldn't be any recruiting at all. I don't know how you would enforce it, though."

Then Bill Foster's memory clicked in with one example of excessive recruiting that he'd been aware of since his high-school days. He had heard that several of the good athletes at his high school in Madison "got guided tours of several colleges with girl escorts." But, he added, "It didn't bother me because I wasn't involved in the sports program."

But big-time sports and their excesses are not limited to the big-time universities—the "mega-versities" that provide educations for thousands and athletic careers for dozens. At Bowdoin College in Maine, the emphasis and tradition are on the academic side of life; but the largest and most heavily used building complex on the campus in Brunswick is the gymnasium.

Yet, lately the faculty has been questioning the athletic program. The college has only 1,100 students, which makes it small and cozy; but football and hockey are recruited fairly heavily, and there are varsity teams in almost every sport. But many of the teachers grumble about a group of "functionally illiterate students" who, they say, cannot write or speak properly. According to the teachers, the cause of the problem is sports—and the acceptance by the college of certain athletes only because they are athletes.

In fact, although most of the athletes at Bowdoin do well in their classes, of the thirty-eight students accepted for remedial tutoring in one school year, twenty-three were student-athletes. To John Denaher, a junior from Grosse Point, Michigan, the irritation is clear: "Most of the athletes here are as bright as everyone else, but there are a few real jerks who somehow got in."

"We will accept the athlete," said Richard Moll, the director of admissions. "Winning in some visible sport charms the alumni to give money. This is a policy handed down to my office."

At a small, academically oriented college like Bowdoin, the students seem more aware of the impact of all-out athletics. One student, Edward Allen, a sophomore from Schenectady, New York, did his homework on the subject and came up quoting chapter and verse.

"The school has gone way too far in recruiting jocks," he said. "The only purpose in having a good hockey team is so the alumni will give more money. Some of the jocks only got into school because of their sport, and it shows. The recruiting will not stop as long as Bowdoin is trying to get $40 million from the alumni within the next 10 years."

Allen's figures were correct, at least. Bowdoin has been working on a capital campaign to increase the college's endowment by $40 million. And, according to some on campus, one obvious way of raising money is to put more and more emphasis on winning teams.

Pride and school spirit are historically involved in attitudes toward college athletics. At Nebraska, the minor annoyance of an occupied parking space or bar stool is overwhelmed by the success of the football team. One co-ed, Cindy Johnson, said, "I'm proud of the football team and so is the state. You can see it when we play. Most students can relate better to football than to classes."

That feeling was not echoed a little farther north at Wisconsin, where students have not experienced a top football team in several years.

"Around here, there is less emphasis on athletic teams than at other schools," observed Kent Novitt, a freshman. "I think athletes are considered to be jocks. The emphasis is more toward the arts. So if the Allman Brothers Band came to campus, there would be infinitely more interest than in any basketball game."

"I think they are more like jocks myself," said another student, Ken Saffren, considering the status of the athletes on campus. "I don't think athletes are heroes because they're good at sports, because a lot of other people are good at a lot of other things. I'd be more inclined to look on some famous author as a hero because I'm majoring in English."

As for school spirit, many students at Wisconsin displayed a marked disdain for the idea—though it is not entirely clear whether their disdain was prompted by the college's slump in football or their own aversion to "anachronistic" things.

"What do you define as school spirit?" asked Harriet Gethertz, taking up the cudgels again. "Rah, rah? Forget it. I'd rather not be in a place that's like that."

Still, the "big two" in the Big Ten are football and basketball, and some students concede that success in either sometimes breeds school spirit. Take Ohio State, where football is king and where Wayne Woodrow Hayes is the prime minister.

He believes in discipline, hard work, good blocking, and four yards of hard-won ground. And he is successful, though some persons seem to disagree with his style and his philosophy. Yet, when you talk sports at Woody Hayes's school, you talk football and Woody Hayes. Both mean great success in the national polls, frequent appearances on the national television screens, and impressive sources of money.

The dissenters from all this success tend to complain about the single-mindedness of their football coach and his program. But one student in Woody's corner was Diane Neal, a twenty-four-year-old co-ed in the nursing program.

"America is as good as it is because of competition," she said. "Competitiveness in recruiting is just a reflection of the competitive atmosphere of this country, one of the great powers of the world. Because a college is a prestige-seeking institution, trying to keep up its name, the school is looking for a certain quality of athlete. You've got to recruit them. Right now, the system of recruiting seems to be working."

She was absolutely right: at Ohio State, it was working full-time. If the means justified the ends, then the concept of finding the talent and lining it up was more justified at Ohio State than at most other universities in the country.

But her thoughts were not echoed by all her fellow students, despite the fact that they filled the stadium on those autumn days when the Buckeyes reigned. Harriet Ganson, a twenty-five-year-old graduate student, said: "I really have a disdain for all the hoopla about Ohio State football. It really doesn't enter into my life. All the attention and scholastic help given the players is not going to help them in the real world—unless they go into football."

If graduate students are not necessarily typical of the campus population, consider Alan Green—a senior majoring in history and a former holder of a swimming scholarship at Ohio State. At twenty-two, he can look back a few years into his past and see some significant changes.

"College sports," he said, "are no longer amateur sports, but they're truly professional. It's a job, and that's what they're hiring you for—to be a cog in a machine. The pressure is here, and you've got to come through.

"I wanted to do well in both scholastics and athletics. There was a lot of pressure to do good—to do damn good—in both. The times I was swimming were world records in the forties. But swimmers then just worked out for an hour and jumped out of the pool. Now a loser says, 'I worked out all the time and I failed.' "

"I liked the competition," he recalled, "but there comes a

point when the coach yells at you: 'You lost, you idiot,' and you don't want to compete, you don't want to do anything."

Part of the pressure that athletes like Alan Green resent, though, comes directly from the habit of winning that their colleges may develop. Then, it becomes more fashionable to sit on the Ohio State side during the Michigan game and to root for the big team.

"I can gloat when Ohio State wins," said William Ditty, a sophomore. "During the football season, if you say you're from the University of Iowa, the first thing people think is, 'Oh, yeah, those sorry Hawkeyes.' "

At College Park, Maryland, people can afford to gloat, too, when the University of Maryland starts marching and scoring. There, basketball is the "in" sport, and the fans were promised a national championship by a new coach several years ago. He even took advertisements in the local newspapers proclaiming his promise and inviting the top high-school players in the country to join the bandwagon as it rolled on to Number One.

It is now several years later, and Maryland has not yet reached Number One. But it has come close. And the adventure of competing and winning in the big leagues has exalted the coach, Lefty Driesell. From the back benches, though, voices of dissent are heard: "It's becoming too much of a big business," said Larry Weisman, a sophomore. And: "How can you build the moral fiber of the university when winning is everything?" asked Rick Sherr, another sophomore.

The same sort of mixed feelings were shown at Holy Cross in Worcester, Massachusetts, where some students said they disliked bigness in sports, decried the evils of heavy recruiting, and despised the "jock" and his mentality—but where other students insisted that the issue was not quite that simple.

"Winning solves everything," said Dan Shaughnessey, a junior. And Doug MacEachen, a senior, reflected that "it's kind of wrong, but when the team's better and more people go to the games, there's a common bond."

Some students who don't share the common bond are the

prize scholars, for whom life on campus is a world apart from the heady life on the college's playing fields. Scholars like Sandy Climan, the genius from Bronx High School of Science who scored 100 in advanced calculus before spinning on to Harvard with his report card. The Moses Malone of the smart set. But there were no planes swooping out of the sky to whisk him to a faraway campus, no rallies in his honor, no signs lettered "We want you, Sandy." Not even a summer job.

"Sure, your bright students resent it," he said, turning to philosophy. "But let's face it—athletes can draw money to a university. People like me couldn't do it unless we discovered a cure for cancer, something like that."

Sandy applied, at a total cost of $115, to six major citadels of learning: Harvard, Amherst, Swarthmore, Yale, Skidmore, and Cornell, in that order of preference. All six accepted him, but all noted that his family's income made him ineligible for financial aid on the basis of need.

"It's no picnic," he reported, not revealing any medical or social secrets. "It's a struggle financially. But at least I was able to pick up a few dollars being in math and science."

He meant a few dollars in prize money. But he still could not help but notice that some members of his generation were picking up educations—or careers in shoulder pads—that were worth a few thousand dollars, and then some.

"It has a lot to do with anti-intellectualism in America," Sandy concluded. "People would rather look at a football game than watch 'Meet the Press.' I guess that isn't going to change."

As his parting shot at the system before heading for Harvard, the one-man think factory wrote and delivered the valedictory address before his high-school graduating class. The subject was "mediocrity in America."

To a lesser degree, two other issues divided the student body at many colleges: the place of sports for women and the growth of the "counter-culture" athlete who rejected the "jock" life style for one of his own choosing.

At Holy Cross a few years ago, Gene Doyle played basketball well enough to be drafted by the New York Nets of the American Basketball Association and the Phoenix Suns of the National Basketball Association when he graduated. He also was a radical chairman of the student government.

Dan Shaughnessey, though, felt that Doyle's actions amounted to a ripping off of the school, which had spent time and money recruiting him, and of the coaches, who had spent a lot of time teaching him to play basketball well enough to be drafted by the pros. To Dan Shaughnessey, it was foolish to be so politically militant because "it's not why the kid's here—he's making a lot of effort go down the drain."

Another Holy Cross student saw the counter-culture athlete as a more preferable type than the run-of-the-mill ballplayer. "The athletes are jocks," said Mike Brault, a senior. "They are the most obnoxious people on campus. They're straight, middle-class, bourgeois, and masochistic."

Also well placed at many colleges. But Gwen Lackey, a sports writer for the Wisconsin daily newspaper, thinks she has seen some change. "There are some liberated athletes, or athletes on the road to liberation," she said, "and I like to think it's spreading. But it's spreading only slowly."

Back at Ohio State, though, Diane Neal added the counterpoint: "If a dude's out to make the big time, he's going to break his back to make it."

As for women's sports, the common cry was that they were still limping along as the poor stepsisters of the men's money sports. More colleges are recruiting girls from high schools, but not for the glamour parts of the program.

"I think the athletic structure forgets that sports are supposed to be a participatory experience instead of a viewing experience," Miss Lackey explained. "As such, every student should be allowed to play what he wants. Unfortunately, that's not true. The most notorious example is women's sports, but minor sports also get shafted.

"Right now, women are under the definition of 'club sports' here, and there is around a $25,000 annual budget to include all club sports. Four teams have to use the same uniforms. Although there seems to be a lot of reasons why women are kept in an inferior place, it just doesn't seem fair to me. Women are people.

"Over the years, athletics has become a sort of proving ground for virility. Not only does the male hierarchy feel insecure about giving some of their money to women, but I think they feel threatened by having women placed on an equal level with men."

To Suzanne Soltis of Ohio State, though, the war between the sexes on campus was inspired by the same thing that inspired the war between the varsities.

"The women athletes would like to have the money the men have now," she figured, "and I think that's just as bad."

The old money game. Team, team, team.

CHAPTER XI

Opiate for the Masses

It had been forty-five years since the landmark report by the Carnegie Foundation for the Advancement of Education, a report that found in 1929 that "college sports have been developed from games played by boys for pleasure into systematic, professionalized athletic contests." Now, in 1974, another group of educators took another look at another generation of college athletes. Their chief purpose was to determine whether an even more searching inquiry should be undertaken—an inquiry into the whole landscape, so to speak.

The findings by the academic "team" were relayed in 1974 to the American Council on Education, which was founded in 1918 and which is composed of national and regional educational associations and universities. Its purpose: "to advance, through voluntary and cooperative action, the cause of education and the establishment and improvement of educational standards, policies and procedures."

Quarterbacking the report was George H. Hanford, on sabbatical leave from his position as executive vice-president of the College Entrance Examination Board. He gave full time to the direction of the project from October, 1973, to April, 1974, surrounded by these members of the team:

Carlos Alvarez, a law student at Duke University, working under the supervision of Professor John Weistart; Robert H. Atwell, president of Pitzer College; Jerry Beasley, doctoral candidate in education at Stanford; Roscoe C. Brown, Jr., director of the Institute of Afro-American Affairs at New York University; Leon Coursey, head of physical education and director of athletics at the University of Maryland, Eastern Shore; Melvin Evans, chairman of physical education at Jackson State College in Mississippi; Robert Green, director of the Center for Urban Studies at Michigan State; Charles D. Henry, head of the department of health, physical education, and recreation at Grambling College in Louisiana; Nell Jackson, assistant director of athletics at Michigan State, and John Loy, professor of sociology and physical education at the University of Massachusetts.

Also, Bernard P. Ireland, former member of the College Board staff and director of admissions at Columbia College; Theodore Lowi, professor of political science at Cornell; Isaac Kramnick, also professor of political science at Cornell; Carl Scheingold, professor of sociology at Cornell; Mary McKeown, Doctor of Education, University of Illinois; Felix Springer, doctoral candidate at Columbia; and Yvonne Wharton, who was Mr. Hanford's assistant at the College Board.

Special consultant help was supplied by Joseph Froomkin, Inc., with Dr. Froomkin directing his firm in analyzing the more general implications for college sports of the proposals before Congress to protect the rights of amateur athletes.

"Campuses in all sections of the country were visited," the report notes. "Large and small; men, and women and coed; two- and four-year; public, independent and church-related. Meetings, conferences and conventions were attended. In the process, contacts were made with trustees, presidents and other administrators; athletic directors, coaches, trainers, athletic department business managers, ticket managers, sports information directors and faculty athletic representatives; faculty members, including sociologists, historians, economists, lawyers, philosophers, political scientists and physical educators; students; college athletes, past and present, men and women; and college sports fans.

"Contacts were also made with appropriate personnel from secondary schools and their athletic associations; the field of television and the world of professional sports; with sportswriters and referees; indeed with anyone who the inquiry team thought might make a contribution."

"Only big-time football is generally revenue-producing," the report states, getting right down to brass tacks and green dollars. "Big-time basketball frequently, but far from always, makes it own financial way. Hockey is in a few but growing number of institutions becoming a revenue-producing sport. With only a very few abnormal exceptions, all other varsity sports, along with non-big-time or low-profile football and most basketball and hockey programs, do not pay their own way. Despite its complexity, this distinction is an important one nonetheless, for the major differences among institutions in their policies and practices with respect to the financing of intercollegiate sports rest upon differing expectations with respect to revenue production by football and basketball."

The report gives the following breakdown by sport and type of institution:

Playing big-time football:	83 public institutions
	48 independent institutions
	131 total
Playing big-time basketball:	130 public institutions
	109 independent institutions
	239 total

What this breakdown reveals, apparently, is that big-time sports, and notably football, are more prevalent at public colleges than at private ones; also, that the further a college is from the "big-time," the more likely it is to be independent.

What does it all mean for the colleges and their students,

athletes and scholars alike? It means this, the American Council on Education was told by the inquiry team in these excerpts from the report:

TRENDS

In financial terms, although some observers predict some relief, the economic crunch on higher education can be expected to continue. In educational terms, the diversity of higher institutions and their content coverage can be expected to expand and move out from the traditional liberal arts core. In socio-political terms, the interests of legislators, women and minorities are forcing a re-evaluation of the role of intercollegiate athletics. In moral terms, the distinction between amateur and professional is disappearing. In socio-institutional terms, although sports as entertainment can be expected to continue to play an increasingly important role in our society, big-time intercollegiate athletics can be expected to keep on losing ground despite instances of deceptive appearances to the contrary.

Evidence of the importance of sports in the United States today abounds. It is generally apparent in newspaper coverage that regularly exceeds that of any other topic, in television programming and the viewing habits of the nation, in the rapid expansion of professional sports, in the public interest in spectaculars like baseball's long-time World Series and football's newer Super Bowl, and in the popularity enjoyed by our big-time sports heroes. In more restricted but no less important terms, it is apparent in the discussions about sports as a means of upward mobility for minorities and the poor, in the attention being given by the women's movement to a call for equal rights in intercollegiate athletics, and in the legislation relating to amateur athletics currently before the Congress.

In traditional economic or financial terms, sports have become big business and those in the counterculture counter with the observation that sports have become capitalism's current substitute for religion as the opiate for the masses.

AMATEUR VERSUS PROFESSIONAL

For purposes of intercollegiate competition, a professional in one sport was until last January (1974) considered a professional in all sports. At that time the rules were changed and now a professional in one sport is an amateur in all others, at least in college competition. It is unlikely, however, that he or she will be allowed to participate in international events. For years it was impossible for amateurs to compete with professionals in tennis but acceptable in golf. Now it is possible in both. An amateur is someone who presumably doesn't get paid for playing; yet what else but a payment for services rendered is a grant-in-aid awarded without reference to need?

Amateurism in its purist form disappeared years ago. It existed when individuals played games for fun, paid their own expenses and were coached by amateurs. In 1929 the definition of amateurism was still clear and unequivocal and it made sense to call for a return to a condition that could be both described and achieved. But events were moving college sports in another direction. Those events included the democratization of secondary and then higher education in the United States. Amateur athletics, at the turn of the century at least, were still very much the privilege of the upper class.

Not strangely, however, athletic talent was found to exist in the middle and lower classes as well; and opportunities were arranged to make it available to college sports programs, for a price. The response to the charges of such practices made in the 1929 report was, however, not to outlaw all professionalism but to legitimize certain aspects of it. Thus, today the definition of amateurism must be couched in degrees of non-professionalism.

However described, the concept remains not only an elusive but a controversial one in an era characterized by the predominance of big-time professional sports. The erstwhile coal mining sons of Pennsylvania and their modern counterparts from the black ghettos of urban America or the ice rinks of Canada can well ask whether amateurism, a privilege of the well-to-do, is consistent with the principle of equality of opportunity. And so might a Commission on Intercollegiate Sports.

ADMISSIONS ATTITUDES

Directors of admissions and of financial aid in institutions having low-profile programs tend not to have any distinctive attitudes toward intercollegiate athletics. The coaches may turn up prospects through their own recruiting efforts and the admissions and financial-aid types are as aware as anybody on campus of the need to have not only good students but good musicians and good debaters and good athletes. They are not particularly concerned because they make the decisions as to which ones get in and get aid.

The results of the inquiry suggest that the situation is different in the big-time. Although lip service is sometimes paid through the appropriate shop, the fact is that the athletic department usually handles the admission of and financial aid to the student-athletes, sometimes on completely different academic standards, always on different aid formulas, and most of the time on a different time schedule.

ATHLETE ATTITUDES

The attitudes of athletes involved in intercollegiate sports are generally favorable toward them. Such negativism as has been expressed comes essentially from three sources: male athletes who have become disillusioned with what they consider their exploitation in the interests of big-time sports, minority (primarily black) athletes who feel that they have been subjected to even more severe exploitation, and women who believe that they have been discriminated against in their intercollegiate athletic programs.

The positive attitude of the generality of athletes appears to reflect their satisfaction with their play experience in an education setting; such opposing negativism as does exist appears to reflect dissatisfaction with working conditions in a commercial setting.

The conclusions drawn from these observations are that, except for the three subgroups noted, intercollegiate athletics provide an important and satisfying experience for participants that should be preserved, that the concerns of the disillusioned, the blacks and women should not be solved by the abolition of college sports, and that one of the primary goals for a national study commission should be to accommodate the concerns of the three groups in developing its recommendations for change.

ALUMNI ATTITUDES

Alumni are held by many to be the root of all evil in intercollegiate athletics. They are said to be primarily responsible for the unhealthy pressure for victory, for overzealous recruiting, for under-the-table favors to athletes, for threatening to withhold their largesse that holds up the athletic department, for the hiring and firing of coaches, and for the firing of a president if they happen to think he is getting in the way of a coach they like.

Such practices exist but they appear to be characteristic of an important, vocal but very small minority of generally older alumni. (More recent graduates at most colleges tend not to take their intercollegiate sports quite so seriously.)

In any event, one hypothesis to be explored in a major study would be that alumni support for intercollegiate athletics may not be as widespread or as strong as a vocal minority would have it appear—or as college presidents seem to fear.

Take the case of football crowds, for instance. There is no city in the United States, except for Los Angeles, which houses both a financially self-supporting college athletic program and a professional football team. In those other cities where big-time college football does co-exist with a professional franchise, it is all too easy to assume that the former's inability to attract capacity crowds is attributable to the defection of its former fans to the play-for-pay ranks. However, the impression gathered in the course of this inquiry is that pro followings have by and large been created new, not stolen from the colleges.

Apparently alumni, as well as the general public, have turned their entertainment attention elsewhere. A few individuals have in fact transferred their allegiance in terms of actual attendance to professional sports. Others, given an interest in football but a willingness to devote only one afternoon of a weekend, spend Saturday or Sunday afternoon before the home tube instead of Saturday afternoon at the college field. And the growing interest in sports participation has attracted still others to the golf course or tennis court as participant in preference to the gridiron as spectator.

PARENTAL ATTITUDES

Secondary school and college personnel alike note increasing pressure from parents of athletically talented young men designed to see that their children are given appropriate exposure to college scouts. For instance, in the case of football they seek to have their offspring play the visible or prestige positions (quarterback, back, end) rather than to be hidden in the middle of the line. College recruiters also observe that many parents treat their children as saleable merchandise, attempting in effect to auction them off to the highest bidder.

Whether such parents are victims of, or contributors to, the growing commercialism in intercollegiate sports, their attitudes bespeak the need for change.

SECONDARY SCHOOL ATTITUDES

In one sense they are to intercollegiate athletics what the latter are to professional sports—and they have been in the business of supplying athletes longer. Up to World War I, in the era of football dominance by the prestige private institutions in the East, many private schools recruited "fifth-year students" not only for the benefit of the schools' won-lost record but also in the interests of providing athletic proving grounds for the colleges which they fed. The prep schools which regularly and openly, to use more modern jargon, red-shirted players for the service academies were a classic case in point well into the post-World War II era.

Between the two world wars, new sources were developed, such as the coal-mining areas of Pennsylvania and the industrial cities of northeastern Ohio. Then the arrival of the jet age made recruiting on a national basis possible.

At the same time, developments at the secondary school level have had their effects as well. In particular the evolution and growth of the large consolidated high school has tended to limit the opportunity for latent talent, "late bloomers" as they are called in college admissions, to develop. The chances for getting on the squad in the first place are simply better in small schools.

From the point of view of teachers and administrators, the most serious effect on the athletes is interference with their education: Their absence from class to meet visiting recruiters, or to go on college-sponsored trips to visit campuses; their distraction from homework by college representatives coming to their houses. One large city high school counselor reported that after winning the state basketball championship, "the team virtually dropped out of school" to deal with the recruiting pressure placed upon them.

Reports abound in the public record and in the N.C.A.A. files of school principals, registrars and teachers who have been pressured to alter grades or transcripts so that athletes who would not otherwise qualify for admission can "have the privilege" of going to college. Guidance counselors frequently complain that they are bypassed as far as the top athletes are concerned and suggest that the coaches who assume the college counseling function for their players are not trained for the task. Some observers even suggest that the latter are indeed improperly motivated in undertaking it. While there is little evidence that high school coaches receive remuneration or other recognition for having steered stars in certain collegiate directions, they do of course, as guidance counselors do, have certain institutions with which they have developed special rapport and about which they feel more secure in referring athletes.

At the same time, however, coaches are under more subtle pressure from intercollegiate athletics. Because high school coaching can be a stepping stone to the college ranks if one is successful, there is tremendous pressure to win. And because one is measured by the quality of his workmanship, there is evidence that some secondary school coaches do in fact put their own career self-interest ahead of their students' in aiming their better players for prestige, big-time colleges on a "full-ride" or grant-in-aid basis. If the lad doesn't make it, that's out of the coach's hands.

The attitude of the nation's schools toward athletics affects and is affected by the attitudes of the communities in which they exist. If there is diversity among the nation's more than 2,500 higher institutions, there are even greater differences among our more than 25,000 schools, differences which make generalizations both difficult and dangerous. Yet the fact remains that some of these schools exist in communities which sponsor little league programs which, with all their benefits and faults, serve to demonstrate to youngsters the importance that adults attach to the world of sports—and in communities out of which comes the win-at-any-cost philosophy which infected the Soap Box Derby—the same philosophy which has been at the root of so many of the problems of intercollegiate athletics over so many years.

FINANCIAL AID

Perhaps the saddest self-commentary by the athletic establishment about the state of its own morality appears in the controversy surrounding the award of financial aid to athletes. At the 1973 N.C.A.A. convention, a proposal was presented calling for the abolition of full-ride grants-in-aid and the adoption of a policy calling for the award of financial aid to student athletes on the basis of need.

Two reasons among others were advanced in support of the proposal. One, it is standard practice with respect to virtually all other students. This argument makes good sense, particularly to those who decry special treatment of athletes. In fact, most people in the educational community but outside the athletic establishment are all for it and can't understand why it is not standard practice in the first place. Two, it saves money. This potential result is attractive to some inside the establishment.

One large, big-time, independent institution visited in the course of the inquiry suggested an experience roughly as follows: Under N.C.A.A. regulations, it could award $600,000 in athletic grants-in-aid. Because it, like most private institutions, has much higher tuition than its public counterparts, it needs considerably more scholarship money to support a given athlete. By not awarding all the grants-in-aid that it was entitled to, and by making some of the awards it did make partial instead of full ones, the institution got by with $400,000. If it had used the formula of the College Scholarship Service for computing need and made its awards on that basis, it would have cost only $200,000.

With two such compelling arguments on its side, why was the proposal rejected? It was turned down in 1973 and again in 1974 because the big-time intercollegiate athletic establishment on balance doesn't trust itself. The argument was that such a policy would generate even more under-the-table payments than now exist. Note not only the admission that they now exist, but also the opinions that the pressure to win is so great that coaches would exceed the need formula and that athletes would accept such awards.

In any event, the issue of grants-in-aid versus aid-based-on-need promises to remain a controversial one.

POLICING ATHLETICS

There are both moral and competitive reasons for the existence of self-imposed legislation in intercollegiate athletics: to keep people honest and to even out the competition.

Public attention tends to focus on the former, and one of the criticisms of the N.C.A.A. picked up early in the course of the inquiry was to the effect that it does not have a large enough investigatory staff to carry out its enforcement responsibility for keeping college sports honest. The critics complain not only that the staff is so busy reacting to charges of violations formally lodged with the N.C.A.A. that it has no opportunity to take an initiative, but also that it is not even large enough to follow up adequately on all the complaints that do come in.

The critics of the "jock establishment" suggest that the N.C.A.A. operation, with the members of the establishment policing themselves, is a farce; and some objective observers, while not as extreme in their reaction, opine that some external investigative agency, less closely identified with the enterprise in the public eye, might be preferable. The supporters of the N.C.A.A. effort counter with the observation that the legal and medical professions, for example, have codes of ethics enforced by the members of them. In turn, other observers point out that some college academic departments, such as chemistry or engineering, are approved both by their faculty peers in the accreditation process and by their respective professional societies, which the N.C.A.A., as an association of institutions and not of individuals, is not.

In both the big-time and low-profile arenas, the many athletic conferences around the country play a significant role, frequently having rules and regulations which, being more stringent or restrictive than the national ones, require local attention. The degree of investigatory responsibility assumed by these groupings and the mechanisms by which they self-regulate themselves vary widely and a commonly heard criticism is that, because the members of a conference are by definition like-minded, there is a tendency to berate each other privately for wicked acts and then sweep it all under the rug in the interests of public conference harmony.

Some observers have suggested as a way around this complaint that the N.C.A.A. investigatory staff be beefed up, in part to respond to conference calls for external investigations.

EXTERNAL CONTROLS

At one point in the history of intercollegiate athletics, excesses on the playing field resulted in intervention from outside—at that point by President Theodore Roosevelt in response to the mayhem that was occurring on the gridiron. He told the nation's colleges and universities to do something about the brutality or he would outlaw football. The N.C.A.A. was founded in 1906 to do the job.

Today external pressure is being brought on intercollegiate athletics in the councils of the U.S. Congress to insure that the rights of individual athletes are protected in the organization of international competition. Government sponsorship of an outside agency (external, that is, to higher education and intercollegiate sports) is a part of virtually all of the pieces of legislation currently being proposed.

Congressional attention has been drawn to intercollegiate athletics as a result of recent incidents growing out of the long-standing feud between the N.C.A.A. and the American Amateur Athletic Union. Congressional concern for amateur sports remains aroused in the interests of national pride.

THE N.C.A.A.-A.A.U. FEUD

A long-time athletic director who served simultaneously on the governing boards of both organizations pointed to the frustrations involved in trying to understand the situation when he said in effect, "It was hard to realize that the bastards those other bastards were talking about are these bastards." Feelings run high, reason does not prevail, personalities dwarf issues, the counter-culture finds both sides greedy and rapacious, and whatever is said here is bound to offend somebody, most likely everybody on all sides of the controversy.

There are documents which suggest that the problem has its roots in the distant past. The A.A.U. is reported to have mishandled Jesse Owens in 1936. The 1929 report suggests that the N.C.A.A. hadn't done too well in its first 19 years. Nevertheless, it would appear that the real troubles have developed since World War II. Until about mid-century, the U.S. Olympic Committee was supported primarily by subventions of like amount from the A.A.U. and the N.C.A.A., and each had roughly the same clout in the governance of the U.S.O.C. At about that time, two events occurred which tended to blow the alliance apart.

First, the U.S.O.C. found that it could successfully raise money on its own and was thus able in effect to declare its independence from its two benefactors. Second, an attempt was made to form a coalition of the N.C.A.A. and the representatives of the independent, non–A.A.U. sponsored sports on the U.S.O.C. in a bid to gain control, for reasons which the N.C.A.A. considered sound and legitimate and which the A.A.U. found arbitrary and unwarranted. The differences continue.

The feud today appears at first glance to be a struggle for the control of amateur athletics in the United States, although this appears to be something of an exaggeration. The A.A.U. is accused of being an anachronism in a college-sports-dominated world, a holdover from the heyday of amateur sports clubs around the turn of the century. The N.C.A.A. is accused of being a power-mad agency of professional college coaches. The A.A.U. is held up as the champion of the individual amateur, while the N.C.A.A. complains that its member colleges train and supply most of the manpower for the Olympics but have no say over who is chosen to compete or who the coaches will be.

Individuals like Douglas MacArthur, James Gavin, Theodore Kheel and William Scranton have been asked to mediate but, while temporary truces have been effected in order to get through successive Olympic Games, the tensions remain stronger than ever. The situation has become so intolerable that the U.S. Congress has a number of bills in the works to deal with the situation, to protect the interests of the individual athlete in the power struggle.

STUDENT FEES

One of the major complaints about intercollegiate athletics comes from the students required to pay a fee to support the costs incurred in connection with varsity teams. Although the practice is far from universal, it has been used by a large number of athletic departments as a means of generating additional income.

For example, the athletic director of one of the institutions visited in the course of the inquiry made no bones of the fact that he had used them to achieve the mandate given him to make his department self-supporting. At that institution, students will for the next thirty years be paying off the cost of the new stadium.

In other instances, the dollars are used as the primary source of revenue in achieving a balanced budget. In some such cases, the fee is simply required and there is no fringe benefit, such as the privileges of getting free admission or of buying tickets to games at reduced prices. In many others, such privileges are offered but students point out that they are still being exploited because they don't all want to take advantage of the opportunity to pay. One of the primary reasons that a major university gave up football was that when, in response to student protest, athletic fees were made voluntary, the financial results were such as to cause the abandonment.

On many other campuses, student fees are charged and administered under the auspices of the student government. On a number of them, there has been a tradition of appropriating some portion of them for the athletic department. In these cases, continued support is in question in part because of general student protest over the special treatment given to intercollegiate athletics and in part because of the need for more dollars to support the large increase in intramural activity.

This process of allocation of student fees is, it turns out, such an important function of student government that, in one state with a strong two-year college program, the student governments on many of its campuses went into hibernation when the state authorities acted to provide public funds to support intercollegiate athletics.

SCHOLARLY INATTENTION

The fact that, as one long-time observer of the college sports scene has noted, intercollegiate "athletics have drifted from the mainstream of American education" is nowhere more apparent than in the lack of attention that has been given to the field by members of faculty departments whose subject matter interest has relevance to the topic.

While a few sociologists, political scientists, philosophers, psychologists, economists, lawyers and doctors with scholarly interest in sports and college athletics were identified (in the inquiry), there were only one or two who could be said to have a primary interest in the field. At the same time, virtually all of the institutional exceptions existed in physical-education-departments-turned-departments-of-sports-sciences-and-leisure-studies at state-teachers-colleges-turned-universities manned by physical-educators-turned-social-scientists. Yet even in these latter instances, however, the introduction of psychological and sociological discourse is relatively a new phenomenon.

If the Marxists are right that sports are the current substitute for religion as the opiate for the masses, then both they and their ideological enemies might do well to ponder seriously the suggestion of one college graduate in the alumni magazine of a well-known higher institution to the effect that it should establish a "College of Sport," in this case to be the current substitute for the School of Divinity.

CHAPTER XII

1929: The Way
It Was

Dartmouth was shocked, Stanford silent, Harvard self-righteously indignant. Brown called the report "false in part, misleading in toto," and Bucknell accused the investigators of breaking faith.

In the Midwest, the Big Ten's athletic commissioner said, "We have nothing to be ashamed of." And at Columbia, where the charges were labeled absurd, the dean in charge of scholarships bellowed, "It is possible to stand so straight as to lean over backwards and bump your head."

The date was Oct. 24, 1929, and the Carnegie Foundation for the Advancement of Teaching had just released its historic study on college athletics. Amid the cries of outrage and denial, a few college presidents showed neither shock nor surprise.

"What is said in the report is true," conceded Dr. G. D. Gossard of Lebanon Valley. "Practically all colleges do it. We are compelled to."

What the colleges were doing then is what they are doing now: recruiting athletes. The educators were reacting to "Bulletin 23," whose publication nearly half a century ago stirred a nation-wide furor. Titled *American College Athletics*, the study took three and one-half years to complete. Based on a survey of 130 colleges and secondary schools, the report's 383 scholarly pages told a lurid story of play-for-pay recruiting corruption in a field "sodden" with commercialism and hypocrisy.

An athletic subsidy was defined as follows: "Any assistance, favor, gift, award, scholarship or concession, direct or indirect, which advantages an athlete because of his athletic ability or reputation and which sets him apart from his fellows in the undergraduate body."

Subsidies, it seems, were as much a part of campus life then as they are now. One of every seven college athletes, the report charged, was subsidized to a point bordering on professionalism. The study, directed by Howard J. Savage, sent shock waves reverberating through the academic community with its documentation of grade-tampering and "slush funds" and overzealous alumni.

No other investigation, past or present, has taken so searching a look at college sports in America, though this was by no means the first time that they had been put under a microscope. Throughout the history of intercollegiate sports, the refrain of the loser has been: "If we only had those guys, we would have won."

Even before the turn of the century, recruiting had become an established practice. As far back as 1905, in the era of ringers and tramp athletes and crippling formations, President Theodore Roosevelt demanded a cleanup of what he called the "brutality" of early-vintage football. One of the first actions of the National Collegiate Athletic Association, formed in 1906, was to outlaw the "flying wedge." In this alignment, at least seven players would form a lethal blocking wedge for the ball carrier by linking arms: three men on each side of the wedge, and a "point man" (usually the heaviest) in front like the tip of an arrow. The resulting carnage was not a pretty sight.

So the flying wedge expired. But sports recruiting thrived. In 1927, President A. Lawrence Lowell of Harvard deplored "spectacular contests" and said that colleges should be more than mere adjuncts to football stadiums. He called for a return to the Greek tradition in which each varsity team would play only one intercollegiate game a year. Administrators listened respectfully, and ignored the proposal.

Then, as now, the campus stirrings could be compared to the rumblings of a volcano that erupts from time to time. Yet no eruption before or since has shaken college sports more convulsively than the Carnegie report that broke at the height of the 1929 football season.

In *The New York Times*, the story started on the front page, and two entire inside pages were filled with summations and reactions. The lead headline, spread over two columns at the top and center, announced: "College Sports Tainted by Bounties, Carnegie Fund Finds in Wide Study." A smaller headline underneath noted that the accused colleges included New York University, Fordham, Columbia, Harvard, and Princeton.

Had it not been for two extraordinary non-sports news developments the previous day, the Carnegie story undoubtedly would have received an even more prominent front-page display. Larger headlines of the *Times* were devoted to a $4-billion paper loss on Wall Street as stock prices crashed in a record decline, and to a report prepared for Mayor James J. Walker calling for a $1-billion program of new bridges, tunnels, and subways to relieve traffic congestion in New York City.

Yet those stories didn't detract from the impact of the Carnegie disclosures. At N.Y.U., the varsity football coach called his troops together and told them to brace themselves.

"I've already read the report," said the late Chick Meehan, "and you're going to be shocked when you see . . . how little you're getting paid."

Meehan had been hired to lead N.Y.U. to football prominence. He did so well that stories used to be told about his wading through six feet of snow in the middle of winter to places like Dean Academy and his bringing back a 220-pound tackle strapped over the hood of his car. This was the "bring 'em back alive" routine that big-time college coaches have had to live with to survive.

But the $50 a month that Meehan's N.Y.U. players supposedly got couldn't compare with some of the other Carnegie wage scales. One Pacific Coast football star, the report alleged, sold his complimentary tickets for $100 before every major game.

The present campus crisis, of course, contains elements not present in 1929: the heavy dependence on black athletes to help balance athletic-department budgets; television revenue, which increasingly tends to place the burden of entertainment on college athletics; and the emergence of women athletes as a major influence.

But the moral issue involved in recruiting hasn't changed. And the Carnegie report makes fascinating reading even forty-six years after its publication. It's all there, especially in the correspondence obtained to document some of the abuses. Names of colleges, sites, and people are deliberately garbled to preserve anonymity, but the messages leave little to the imagination. We read of clandestine recruiting trips, of subsidized freshmen who "will be bearcats" on the varsity football team, of high-school athletes to be "taken care of, same as the others," of "big strapping boys" raking leaves on the campuses, of athletic directors who work twelve to fifteen hours a day and are "just bubbling over with enthusiasm" for their programs, of eager townspeople and "old pendulums" about to swing in the direction of one college or another.

The importance of college athletics in what the report called "this game of publicity desired by the university" was reflected in the same Thursday issue of *The New York Times* that carried the Carnegie recruiting charges. On two pages, each topped by an eight-column headline, dispatches of varying length from forty-six campuses throughout the nation reported up-to-the-minute football developments.

In New Haven, one of the few places where evidence of recruiting abuses had not been found, Albie Booth of Yale had run eighty yards for the only touchdown as the varsity tuned up for the Army game with a 7-0 victory over the freshmen. From Cambridge came word that Ben Ticknor of Harvard was ill and would miss Saturday's game with Dartmouth. Princeton faced a "crucial test" against Navy, its coach warned, and Penn made a "sweeping shake-up" in its line for the Lehigh game.

Columbia had scrimmaged against the Manhattan freshmen at Baker Field, and at N.Y.U., Coach Meehan said the Violets would not use their star quarterback, Dave Myers, a black student, in the Nov. 9 game with Georgia at Yankee Stadium.

"We understood the feelings of southern colleges in regard to playing against Negroes," Meehan was quoted as saying, "and the name of Myers did not enter into the negotiations with Georgia."

From South Bend, Indiana, the dispatch in the *Times* of Oct. 24 reported that Notre Dame's ailing coach, Knute Rockne, had watched the team practice and would accompany it to Pittsburgh for Saturday's game with Carnegie Tech. And from Evanston, Illinois, the word was that Northwestern's 50,000-seat stadium had been sold out for upcoming games with Illinois and Notre Dame.

It was against this background that the Carnegie accusations exploded. In its Preface, the report raised two basic questions about the role of organized athletics in American college life:

"What relation has this astonishing athletic display to the work of an intellectual agency like a university?"

"How do students, devoted to study, find either the time or the money to stage so costly a performance?"

Against a contemporary background of deepening campus crisis, educators are beginning to ask those same questions again.

Following are excerpts from the 1929 Carnegie report, *American College Athletics*:

PREFACE*

*Athletics, an Element in the Evolution of the
American University*

Instead of holding the universities in contempt, we ought
rather to endeavor to recall them to more sober studies.
Erasmus to Luther, May, 1519

---

* Additional material on this report appears in Appendix I, p. 179.

While the university in every civilized country will reflect, to a greater or less extent, national ideals and habits of mind, its primary function in every country is to serve as an exponent of its highest intellectual life. This is the reason and the justification for its existence and the basis of its appeal for support.

II

Nothing in the educational regime of our higher institutions perplexes the European visitor so much as the role that organized athletics play. On a crisp November afternoon he finds many thousands of men and women, gathered in a great amphitheater, wildly cheering a group of athletes who are described to him as playing a game of football, but who seem to the visitor to be engaged in a battle. . . . At the end, the vast majority of the onlookers only know, like old Kaspar of Blenheim, that " 't was a famous victory" for one university or the other.

When the visitor from the European university has pondered the matter, he comes to his American university colleagues with two questions:

"What relation has this astonishing athletic display to the work of an intellectual agency like a university?"

"How do students, devoted to study, find either the time or the money to stage so costly a performance?"

III

It has been assumed that there is a legitimate place in the secondary school and in the college for organized sports, that such sports contribute, when employed in a rational way, to the development both of character and of health. The report is a friendly effort to help toward a wise solution as to the place of such sports in our educational system. It has been necessary, in order to render this service, to set forth the abuses and excesses that have grown up.

XV

It goes without saying that 50,000 people (not an unusual attendance) could not be gathered to witness a football game through the mere pull of college loyalty or interest in the sport. The bulk of the spectators do not understand the game. They are drawn to this spectacle through widespread and continuous publicity.

In no other nation of the world will a college boy find his photograph in the metropolitan paper because he plays on a college team. All this is part of the newspaper effort to reach the advertiser.

Into this game of publicity the university of the present day enters eagerly. It desires for itself the publicity that the newspapers can supply. It wants students, it wants popularity, but above all it wants money and always more money.

The athlete is the most available publicity material the college has. A great scientific discovery will make good press material for a few days, but nothing to compare to that of the performance of a first-class athlete. Thousands are interested in the athlete all the time, while the scientist is at best only a passing show. And so it happens that the athlete lives in the white light of publicity.

XVII

What ought to be done?

The paid coach, the gate receipts, the special training tables, the costly sweaters and extensive journeys in special Pullman cars, the recruiting from the high school, the demoralizing publicity showered on the players, the devotion of an undue proportion of time to training, the devices for putting a desirable athlete, but a weak scholar, across the hurdles of the examinations—these ought to stop and the inter-college and intramural sports be brought back to a stage in which they can be enjoyed by large numbers of students and where they do not involve an expenditure of time and money wholly at variance with any ideal of honest study.

When the intellectual life of a body of college students is on a low plane, the difference between the formal credits of men in training for inter-college contests and those of the ordinary student who is not in training may be inappreciable. But it requires no tabulation of statistics to prove that the young athlete who gives himself for months, body and soul, to training under a professional coach for a gruelling contest, staged to focus the attention of thousands of people, and upon which many thousands of dollars will be staked, will find no time or energy for any serious intellectual effort.

The need today is to re-examine our educational regime with the determination to attain in greater measure the simplicity, sincerity, and thoroughness that is the life blood of a true university in any country at any age.

The Money Appraisal of Games

It is highly improbable that many schoolboys or schoolgirls who have not been subject to older influences would spontaneously appraise athletic contests in terms of their return in dollars. Those cases in which the financial profits from athletics have been used in materially enriching organizations or in providing buildings and playing fields, with the consequent easing of the taxpayers' burden, reveal the tampering of older persons.

Commercialism cuts both ways. It destroys youth's discernment of true values and intentions, and it depreciates the worth of the very device that engendered it. Continually appraise athletic performance at a price, and all that contributes to it and honors it has also its price.

Scholastic Abuses and Athletics

Grades assigned by school teachers for particular courses are known to have been raised by certifying officers on solicitation of college coaches or alumni in order to enable boys to slip easily into college.

The Effects Upon the Schoolboy

The principal sufferers from the policy of separating athletics and physical education in many public schools are the body of youth whom it touches. If it were necessary to sum up in a single phrase the worst results of that separation, probably that phrase would be the impairment of ethical and moral standards of schoolboys through the commercialization of athletics.

Of a number of cases that have been collected, one will illustrate almost all of the abuses to which the divorce of athletics from physical education in schools can lead: the secret payment of money for athletic participation, physical violence, and dishonesty.

In a large Eastern city there recently arose an angry controversy over the eligibility of a school athlete on the ground of age. Although the athlete, his father, and a clergyman all maintained the boy was eligible, a public school official, being led by virtue of his office to investigate, concluded from records of the athlete in a neighboring state, as well as from local documents, that the boy's age was being misrepresented and that he was too old to participate under the rules. The official presented these facts to a meeting of the local athletic committee and the boy was declared ineligible.

On leaving this meeting the school official was confronted by the young man's father, who demanded, "Why have you interfered with my boy's education?" The official replied that he was merely carrying out regulations. Without warning, the parent struck the official. Just then the boy appeared and expressed his desire to "take a crack" at the official, too. Thereupon the official threw down his armful of books, his overcoat and various other encumbrances, seized a chair, and stood his ground.

Assistance to School Athletes

Our study has revealed arrangements between college coaches on the one hand and high school and academy coaches on the other, whereby, all unknown to the authorities of either school or college, promising athletic material is passed on from one to the other. It is generally the college alumnus with a distorted sense of values who recruits public high school boys for preparatory schools with a view of getting them ultimately to play upon university teams.

"Shopping Round"

"Shopping round" is the soliciting by a prospective college athlete of financial assistance in the form of a scholarship or other aid at a college or a private school in exchange for athletic participation, in such a fashion that the offers, real or imagined, from one institution are used to procure offers or overtures from another. Perhaps the most important single result of "shopping round" upon the schoolboy's character is the engendering of a purely materialistic attitude at an age when his outlook upon life is naturally quite the opposite.

Maintenance of Academic Standing

For practical purposes, there appears to be little difference between this practice [professional tutoring for athletes] and relieving a regular salaried member of the athletic staff from some of his other duties in order that he may supervise the academic standing of athletes.

Subsidies without Athletic Scholarships

Alumni subsidies are dispensed, sometimes by a member of the athletic staff or someone intimately connected with athletics, from a "slush fund" or "black box fund," and thus a close supervision of beneficiaries can be maintained.

In an extreme case of subsidizing, alumni and businessmen made contributions ranging from $10 to nearly $1,000 annually to a fund aggregating from $25,000 to $50,000 a year. Additional sums, termed "pay checks," were distributed to leading performers.

Complimentary Tickets as Subsidies

It is common practice, particularly among certain football players, to sell the complimentary tickets allotted to them as members of squads. A football player at a university on the Pacific Coast sold his allotment at a profit of about $100 each for various major games of a single season.

Summary

The bearing of subsidizing upon the amateur status comes down at last to a question of motive. No matter what the source of the subsidy, if the reason behind it can be accurately determined, the status of the athlete becomes at once clear. Any favor, however small, that tends to assist an athlete financially, if it is done because he is an athlete, marks the beginning of professionalism. There is no valid reason why even the most worthy athlete should receive any consideration, favor, assistance, or attention that is not available, upon the same terms and with the same readiness, to the general body of undergraduates. Nor is it easy to see how the sincere amateur could expect such special consideration or advantage.

The Press and College Athletics

Sports have grown to an unprecedented importance as news. On the whole, this emphasis has proved profitable to newspapers as regards both the influence and the respect in which they are held, and also the advertising carried on the sporting pages. The extraordinary growth of the sporting page has led to the charge that newspapers are exploiting college and school athletics for financial gain. Nor is this accusation directed against the daily press alone; it extends to monthly magazines and weekly publications. In sports writing, as in other phases of newspaper work, sensationalism almost always originates in a deliberate policy of magnifying the supposed interest or emotional connotations of facts beyond the proportions that their intrinsic values justify.

Conclusion on Recruiting

The foregoing exposition attempts to penetrate the deepest shadow that darkens American college and school athletics. Yet in the murk there are many brighter patches. The absence of recruiting and of subsidizing at many institutions, the integrity of the men who have struggled against these evils with varying degrees of success, the unassailable fact that neither subsidizing nor recruiting is essential to college sport, and the improvement that has been manifest in these particulars during the last quarter-century should hearten anyone who is battling against the corruptions here shown or deplores these perversions of common honesty.

This much is certain: The university or college that, under capable leadership, makes up its collective mind to cast out these practices, can do so. What is needed is constancy of purpose and patience in the face of opposition from those whose self-interest, false pride, and mistaken loyalties make their recession difficult.

Experience has shown that, of all who are involved in these evils— administrative officers, teachers, directors of athletics, coaches, alumni, undergraduates, and townsmen—the man who is the most likely to succeed in uprooting the evils of recruiting and subsidizing is the college president. It is his duty to coordinate opinion and direct the progress of an institution. If neighboring presidents are like-minded, his task is a little lightened, but under no circumstances which we have been able to discover is it impossible even if he stands alone. It cannot be easy. But such are the position and the powers of the American college president that, once having informed himself of the facts, and being possessed of the requisite ability and courage, he will succeed.

[Following are letters cited in the Carnegie report on recruiting, with names purposely garbled in capital letters by the authors of the report.]

A SCHOOL COACH PLACES AN ATHLETE

Dear FBJM:

This will introduce you to JZFG, who played end here last two years. JZFG will be one of your regular varsity men with a year on freshman team. Weighs 178 stripped, 19 years old. If you cannot fix him up same as other men why look after him with full tuition and a job for board and room waiting on table as he is willing to work for board and room. Best of luck.

Yours truly,
CKOH

AN ALUMNUS RECEIVES INSTRUCTIONS

Dear XGZH:

Referring to your letter to Coach LJGDZ relative to MBCET OUTEQ, we certainly are interested in seeing him at KUHTF College. I believe that there is only one way to get OUTEQ interested to the extent that he will want to be in school here and that is to have him on the campus some time this spring, the sooner the better. It does not look any too well to send someone from here to get him and bring him back.

I believe that the best way to bring OUTEQ to the campus is for you to bring him here and then take him back with you. In this way he is merely making a trip with you and we are protecting ourselves at the same time. I will, of course, take care of any expenses which you may incur for the trip. I will appreciate very much an early answer and trust that you can arrange to bring him down at an early date. Bring him any time you can get away, a weekend would be better of course.

Hoping to see you soon, I am

Sincerely yours,
[General Manager]

A RECRUITING ENTERPRISE

Dear Mr. ZCBM:

Your letter has been turned over to me, since I am the representative for the purpose of looking up football material for the coming year. I am very glad that you are interested in MNBF College and I feel sure you will never regret it if you make up your mind to come to MNBF. With best wishes, I beg to remain,

Sincerely yours,
[Freshman Coach]

A RECRUITER APPROACHES A COLLEGE TEACHER

Dear Mr. GFLS:

I am writing to you concerning a Freshman now at SFHK by the name of LOKU whom you had in Freshman English this year. As you know, LOKU is one of three men in the Freshman class to receive numerals in three major sports . . . I wonder, Mr. GFLS, if you are thoroughly acquainted with LOKU's position in regard to finances. LOKU at SFHK on a scholarship . . . He cannot look to home for any financial aid due to the fact that his father is dead and his mother is working for a big lawyer in Boston who is a SFHK man . . .

For that reason, Mr. GFLS, I am taking the liberty of cashing in on a personal connection which I believe to have with you, and writing to you to see if it will be at all possible for you to re-examine LOKU's paper and if at all possible pass him in this course . . .

I have recently done quite a little business in HLFS, both at the . . . National Bank with Mr. LURF MBDE, and at the . . . Savings Bank with Mr. EQSH, and in the event that you should see them please extend to them my very best regards.

With kind personal regards to you, I am

Very truly yours,
K. D. KQEO

THE COLLEGE TEACHER REPLIES

Dear Mr. KQEO:

Regarding LOKU—I shall be willing to re-examine his examination book, although it will not be possible for me to do it until September. Frankly, I doubt if any re-reading will result in changing his grade. He had a low term average, and his examination paper was decidedly poor . . . I am inclined to think the greatest liberality should be shown in LOKU's case and that even with a condition in English, he should be allowed to retain his scholarship and go on with his work . . . But I don't think that the standards of the English Department can rightly be lowered to compromise the case of one man.

Sincerely yours,
LINF Q. GFLS

A RECRUITER REPORTS TO AN ALUMNUS

Dear Sir:

ODS IFSK, the four boys and I left CDGF Friday morning—spending the night in DYKD and arriving in JQEK Saturday noon. UKH QECH, Mr.

OKGB's assistant, met us royally and had arranged meals and beds for us at the DNK LWK House. Two DYKD Alumni were also in town for the weekend with four boys . . .

Then followed a very good baseball game with HLGF EZJD, our team winning 5-3 against the pitching of DeSzow's son. While we were winning that day in baseball, our track team was trimming KHYD at JFSX, our golf team beating LIHF, and our tennis team on top in their game—so it was a big SKWD day . . .

That evening while our four boys were being entertained at the DNK LWK House, ODS and I were invited to dine with Mr. and Mrs. OKGB. He certainly is a bundle of energy—working about 12-15 hours a day, just bubbling over with enthusiasm for SKWD and his program every minute. Every one on the Campus is for him—the townspeople, the people all through the state have all felt the influence of his wonderful personality and are all awake and up and at 'em, which is certainly a new atmosphere in JQEK. He introduced us to a big, strapping, nice looking boy named KDOC, who was working in the house and yard that day. Just a year ago one of our Alumni in DOCG drove with KDOC to JQEK. Result: he enters school last Fall, was a bear cat on the Freshman team—is working his way through school—and if ever I saw a boy with real SKWD spirit, he is the one. He tells me he is bringing three others from DOCG with him next fall.

I can't help but feel that the old pendulum has started to swing our way—bound to result in a better athletic situation, and a bigger and better university. Our Alumni Association in DYKD has raised a fund of $2,500 for the purpose of taking DYKD boys to JQEK with an idea of interesting them in the school . . . I will return to our treasurer a small balance which I hope will be conserved for a future trip of similar nature.

Yours very truly,
BEJO J. TIGK

CHAPTER XIII

The Class of 1974, Inc.

There has never been any sure way of getting into college, but in 1974 it didn't hurt to be Chris Legree.

Chris Legree? Ask any scout. Any of the scouts, in fact, for the 200 colleges that took the time and trouble to get in touch with Chris Legree in order to advise him that he was *the* athlete for them and to explain why they were the college for him. These scouts would tell you that he was quarterback on the football team of Brooklyn's South Shore High School, one of the largest public high schools in the United States, and runner-up for the championship of the Public Schools Athletic League; pitcher for the baseball team in the P.S.A.L. championship finals; and letter man for two years in basketball.

In short, the member of the Class of 1974 voted by all those scouts as most likely to succeed.

Chris was good in baseball and basketball, all right. But he was labeled "great" in football, perhaps the best player from a public high school in New York City since John Brockington graduated from Thomas Jefferson High in Brooklyn ten years earlier and headed toward the Green Bay Packers.

Chris Legree could accurately hurl a football sixty yards; he directed a team of seventeen-year-olds with a coolness that none of his teammates could match; he was bright, good-looking, and quick with the smile. He was also black and street-wise—ghetto streets, at that. He gave evidence that he could handle the burdens of public attention, including the ink he kept getting in major newspapers and magazines. He displayed extraordinary confidence in his ability and in himself. Although the term "capacity for All-America ranking" has been overworked, it certainly applied to Chris for a number of reasons.

One thing he was not: a good student. But in 1974 that did not discourage the waves of colleges beating a path to his doorstep in a ghetto of Brooklyn. Weak scholar, strong quarterback. He could make any college famous, and he probably could make most colleges a heap of money.

One of Chris Legree's classmates at South Shore High, tucked away in the shadows of the Class of '74, was Robert Gerber. A world apart from the tumultuous scene surrounding Chris on the gridiron, basketball court, and diamond, Robert Gerber was merely the best student at South Shore High. He was aiming for a career as a doctor and he had an average of 98 to back up his aim.

Unfortunately for Robert, though, it would have been very difficult in 1974 for him to make any college famous or rich, except from his tuition fees. Brains were just not "in." Athletic ability *was* "in." So Robert graduated from a system that has produced more brilliant students than brilliant quarterbacks, but a system that has rewarded colleges far more for acquiring one outstanding quarterback than it has for acquiring 100 outstanding students.

One day during their senior year, Chris Legree and Robert Gerber met—for the first time—to discuss their experiences in the Class of 1974 and to rap about what it was like to be seventeen and preparing for college. They had been attending classes in the same school and floating around the same hallways term after term, but this was the first time that the top athlete and the top

Big men on campus of South Shore High School in Brooklyn: Robert Gerber, class valedictorian, holding book, and Chris Legree, star quarterback, holding football. Worlds apart, they had never met until they posed for this picture.

scholar at South Shore High had ever shaken hands with each other. And even then, the encounter was arranged by a curious outsider who was examining the curious values of education in the 1970s.

Robert, remarkably, didn't feel cheated by the fact that an athlete ranked as such a prize for so many institutions of higher learning. "I guess the schools want well-rounded student bodies," he suggested, not intending the pun or the insight. Still, he couldn't ignore the realities of the situation, chiefly the reality of publicity.

"The colleges know where to look for athletes," he ventured, showing some of his classroom acumen, "because of their publicity. A good student has to come to them. I've been going after them, they don't come to me. I'm looking at schools that can help me become a doctor. I just hope to get into a school where I'd fit in and be happy."

Another consideration, in one word, was money. Robert Gerber's family was part of the great middle class—too "rich" to get help but "poor" enough to need it. If the financial strain of paying $5,000 or $6,000 a year seemed too burdensome, he might always settle for a state college. But his four leading choices were Harvard, Princeton, Brandeis, and Rochester.

So in 1974 he was a young man who had spent his high-school years becoming the best student that he could become, and that was outrageously good, indeed. Yet he stood talking it all over, wondering and even worrying where he might find an open door to the eventual Class of 1978 at the next level of his education.

Chris was surprised to hear that. Most of his friends were athletes or guys from the neighborhood. None of them was a class valedictorian with a 98 average. Chris confessed that he felt "bad that a kid with a 98 average can't pick his school." Then he added a little wistfully, "If I had a 98 average and my ability as a player, I'd tell them when and where I'd go."

But Chris was not overly modest, so the reality of the situation became clear to him, too. "I've gotten publicity for things I do," he said, "and I think it's right that for my hard work in football, my reward is to pick my school."

To understand the tremendous difference between the super athlete and the super student, let's take a background tour through the worlds of Chris Legree and Robert Gerber.

They came to the high school in Canarsie with differing outlooks and goals. Chris dreamed of becoming the best athlete in the city, but beyond that goal things weren't too clear. He didn't expect to become a professional football player; yet he grew a little dreamy when he talked about it, and he left no doubt that his "main man" was Joe Namath. It was hard not to dream of Shea Stadium if you were poor and black, and if you had started playing football on Osborne Street in Brownsville.

"I think that's what made me such a good player," Chris said. "You have to be good to dodge cars, broken glass, and the other team in a two-hand-touch game in the gutter."

He talked vaguely about college as an escape from ghetto life and all its obstacles, but he doubted that he would desert his home turf altogether. He figured that he would return one day to work in the ghetto and help other young people make their way out.

Robert hadn't thought much of becoming Number One in his own field before he arrived in high school. In fact, it wasn't until his senior year that he established himself in that spot. But he knew all along where it might carry him: to medical school and his career as a doctor. He looked on college as a way of escaping his environment, too. He wanted to leave Brooklyn and meet new, different people, and that desire was perked up by a summer spent on a project for future doctors.

Robert calculated that he spent twenty hours a week on his school work: calculus, advanced biology, physics, and English. That was his load in his final term in high school, when someone with his marks could be "winding down" and sort of coasting to graduation. He made it clear that he wasn't just "a mole who spends all my time in the house." He also liked horseback riding, sports among friends, and class shows.

Chris left the basketball team during his senior year to spend more time studying. He said that, even if he didn't get an athletic scholarship, he would still go to college, because one of his goals was to "hand that diploma to my mother." But despite that noble goal, he knew that he hadn't applied himself as he should have in the classroom. He put in about ten hours a week on courses in Spanish, economics, American history, and English. In college, he said, he hoped to be more successful in combining football with academic effort.

"I know I can do better academically," he said. But again, his confidence helped him ride out the situation. He let the college recruiters know that "I want to be a quarterback—I think I can play big-time quarterback. The key is progress."

While his progress academically was a little stunted, his progress athletically was remarkable. He went from the glass-strewn streets in Brownsville out to Shea Stadium before one of the Jets' games. There he met—and played catch with—his "main man,"

Joe Willie Namath. That opportunity, he conceded, was the choicest part of a larger adventure: being the subject of an article in a national magazine.

Talking about their past and some of their future, both Chris and Robert learned something that day about how the other half lives. And Chris probably surprised Robert when he expressed some mixed feelings about his stature as a "star."

"People come up to me and say, 'Why you so sad?' " Chris said. "Well, I look sad, but I'm not. I just want to prove I can be a success two ways. I can't accept success until I prove myself academically."

He felt good, he went on, when he was playing football in the street, and the younger boys looked up to him and even listened to him. "What I do means something to them," he allowed. "Kids even ask me for my autograph. But I don't want people to envy me."

Then he pointed to Robert Gerber and said: "I hope some people look up to him and say, 'I'd like to be like him.' "

But not many kids were asking Robert for his autograph in the streets. Nor, for that matter, were they asking another member of the Class of '74 at another school: Pierre Davis of Bayside High in Queens. If Chris Legree was the Number One football player in the city, then Pierre Davis was Number Two—maybe even Number One and one-half. He scored seven touchdowns in one game as a senior, he finished the season with 142 points, and his team beat Legree's for the public-school championship. With statistics like those to write on a college application, Pierre Davis believed the recruiters would be knocking down the gates to sign him. At least, he had more in common with Chris Legree than with Robert Gerber.

But, in one of those strange twists of fate, Pierre won almost nothing in the recruiting wars. It was like spending days and nights preparing for the big holiday feast for the family, then settling back, waiting for the doorbell to ring—and having nobody come. Pierre set his table with all those fancy statistics, but the best he could produce in the recruiting feast was a couple of partial scholarship offers—the kind that don't promise anything if you don't make the team or become injured or are unable to stick.

Why was Chris Legree able to ride his talented right arm into almost any school he chose, while Pierre Davis was left standing on his talented football feet? Two sets of numbers supplied the answer: Pierre was rather small to be a running back at a major college, and his speed was not good enough to compensate for his lack of size. In high school, he did his running behind a remarkably capable front line, one that wiped out its competition nearly every week. He also was surrounded by other good runners who took some pressure off him. He was talented—but so were hundreds of other seniors around the country, and not with a slide rule as in Robert Gerber's case. At 5-feet-9 and 180 pounds, Pierre Davis just didn't seem like a very good risk to the recruiters.

That was one set of minus numbers. The other set consisted of his classroom grades. They held him back more than any high-school linebacker ever did. Before enrolling at Bayside, where his brother was a student, Pierre attended Andrew Jackson High, another school in Queens. When he was a freshman, his father was killed—murdered. Pierre, already not an outstanding student, rapidly became even less outstanding. He ignored school, and his grades tumbled.

"I used to clown around," he recalled, "but then in my junior year, it hit me." What hit him was the realization that his grades were going to anchor his feet firmly into ghetto life and all its problems, unless he could turn things around.

"If you get down," he reasoned, "and say I'm gonna do this, you have to have the willpower to do it. You have to blame yourself if something goes wrong. It's like loving candy and then you have to give it up. I had to quit clowning and get my grades up."

Pierre's grades came up, but not far enough up. The failing grades from Jackson High followed him and haunted him at Bayside. "West Virginia asked me to sign a letter," he remembered, "and that would guarantee a scholarship." He didn't say if that happened before or after West Virginia checked his grades closely, but the offer was later withdrawn. He had become too big a risk.

"I don't count how many letters I got from colleges," he said, but the fact was that he was not very heavily recruited. "I didn't know about writing letters to schools and selling myself," he said.

Pierre did have one thing going for him, something that Robert Gerber didn't have going for him. His coach was Neal Nelson, a man who had long since decided that his high-school stars were not necessarily the best football players in the land: Notre Dame doesn't always want a lineman just because he plays on the championship team in New York City. After being big fish in little ponds, high-school athletes swim upstream and become little fish in the big ponds of college sports. So Neal Nelson sent football players to colleges like Guilford in North Carolina and Minot in North Dakota. If they fitted in, played some ball, and got an education, they would be reasonably happy people. Nelson understood that; his problem was getting his athletes to understand it.

"I feel I could start with anybody," Pierre lamented, joining the majority of those who did not understand. But his conviction was not widely shared as the recruiters made their pitches and the top-grade talent made their choices.

To complicate matters, Pierre almost became the victim of some outside "help." One of his relatives went on a one-man campaign for Pierre, because he felt strongly that the boy wasn't getting a fair shake. The man said this to Nelson in so many words. Then he said that Nelson had refused to help, so he called the chancellor of the Board of Education and *The New York Times*. He charged that the coaches were thoughtless, he insisted that coaches in other places went out of their way to help their athletes, and he asked if something couldn't be done for Pierre.

"He called me," Coach Nelson said later, giving a different version, "and said, 'Everyone else is doing it. All you have to do is change those marks and he'll be able to go wherever he wants.' "

The fact was that not everyone was doing it; at least, not everyone was being caught doing it. Oklahoma got caught and wound up on two years of probation imposed by the National

Collegiate Athletic Association. The Sooners got their quarterback from a high school in Texas, but they paid the price: no television appearances and no bowl appearances for two years.

"I told him," Nelson said, "that I would do everything to help Pierre. But that didn't include changing his marks. The kid didn't project a 2.0. I called a friend of mine at Illinois about Pierre, and they were interested in him until they saw his grades. He failed all his subjects at Jackson."

A classmate of Davis's at Bayside High was the best swimmer in the public schools. He had problems, too. He was Doug Landau, and he had something going for him besides his ability in the pool: he was a good student. A good student and a good swimmer. Not a good enough swimmer to get a free ride at a big-time college, but good enough to draw an offer from St. John's: four years in the pool, courtesy of the college. But St. John's was only a short bus ride from home, and you don't want to stay home to attend college. A full scholarship is tempting, but this is your life and choosing a college is one of the most critical decisions you'll make in it.

"I'm under pressure from my parents," admitted Doug, who had been under plenty of pressure as the city champion in the 100-yard breast stroke. "It's hard to pass up a full scholarship at St. John's. But when I pick my school, it will be mainly on cost and academics. Swimming would be third."

His true choice was Columbia. In New York, yes; but far enough away from his home to satisfy his need to "get away" to a college, because he would stay in a dormitory. The rub was that his grades were high but not high enough, probably, for Columbia. And beyond that, he acknowledged, "I'd never make it if it weren't for swimming."

So he stood and frowned, like Robert Gerber and Pierre Davis. He was a middle-class type with some academic assets; but he didn't particularly want a scholarship worth about $20,000, because it wasn't just right for the next four years of his life.

Surrounding all these "problem children" of 1974 were the

masses of seniors who felt the pressure of college without the exhilaration of being either star athletes or star students. Like Mitch Rubinstein of Columbus High in the Bronx.

"When I apply to a college," he complained, "they never see me. All they see is a piece of paper. They look at my marks and say I can go there or I can't. They don't check my background to find out if I had some problem that brought my marks down. They'd do those things if I were an athlete."

If he were an athlete, they might do a lot of things to ease his way into college. Some of them, in fact, were outlined in a letter from the director of a high-school basketball tournament on Long Island to college coaches who never heard of Mitch Rubinstein:

> "Dear Coach: We want to invite you to one of the country's premier high-school attractions—New York's Top 8 Classic—to be played March 21, 22, 23, 24 at Hofstra University on Long Island."

The next two paragraphs listed the eight teams involved and extolled their virtues. They were among the best high-school basketball teams in New York State in 1974. Then the letter told the coaches the real reasons for the correspondence:

> "As you all know, a number of outstanding prep stars are on these teams, and we know that all of you see the recruiting value in attending this tournament.

"For $50 we are giving all college coaches:
  1. Two tickets for each session.
  2. Free entrance to the hospitality room each day.
  3. Two tickets to the post-tournament buffet.
  4. Public address introductions to the entire crowd.
  5. An acknowledgement in the tournament journal as a 'College Booster.'
  6. Will help to introduce you to players, coaches, or parents. We are encouraging them to use and meet in the hospitality room."

(*The New York Times/William E. Sauro*)
Key people in the sports boom of the Seventies: cheerleaders, 180 strong, undergo intensive training at Monmouth College in New Jersey, learning their role in the way of life surrounding college athletics.

For their pains, though, the organizers of the Top 8 tournament almost wound up without a basketball court. When the letter was printed in *The New York Times*, the N.C.A.A. called Hofstra. No member could be associated with the event, the college was told, and the Top 8 could not use the Hofstra gymnasium.

With apologies to those offended—but without money from the colleges warned—the tournament finally went on as scheduled. But that didn't solve anything for Mitch Rubinstein or Pierre Davis or Doug Landau. Or Chris Legree or Robert Gerber, the two "best" at South Shore High, who had never crossed paths until they were trapped by their college crisis in the springtime of their senior year. Or for anybody else in the bedazzled, besieged, and bewildered Class of 1974.

Appendix I

AMERICAN COLLEGE ATHLETICS

*The Carnegie Foundation
for the Advancement of Teaching*

EXTRACT FROM PREFACE TO THE REPORT OF 1929

In the United States, the composite institution called a university is doubtless still an intellectual agency. But it is also a social, a commercial and an athletic agency, and these activities have in recent years appreciably overshadowed the intellectual life for which the university is assumed to exist.

In the second place, the football contest that so astonishes the foreign visitor is not a student's game, as it once was. It is a highly organized commercial enterprise. The athletes who take part in it have come up through years of training; they are commanded by professional coaches; little if any personal initiative of ordinary play is left to the player. The great matches are highly profitable enterprises. Sometimes the profits go to finance college sports, sometimes to pay the cost of the sports amphitheater; in some cases the college authorities take a slice of the profits for college buildings.

The process by which football has been transformed from a game played by boys into a profitable professional enterprise can only be understood by a review of the transformation of the American college of fifty years ago into the present-day American university.

Fifty years ago our highest institutions of learning called themselves colleges. Their courses of study were not so widespread as they are today, but the college conceived of itself as an intellectual agency. To train the habits and the powers of mind was its function. All other matters were incidental to this fundamental purpose.

Students began with certain required studies. In our oldest college, Harvard, the freshman of fifty years ago was required to study Greek, Latin, mathematics, a foreign language and certain scientific studies, generally chemistry or physics. Many electives were offered in the following years.

About this time, colleges in the United States began to be sensitive over the fact that they were not on a plane of scholarship and research comparable with that of the European universities, and particularly of the German universities to which American students were beginning to resort in increasing numbers. The American college did not pretend to be a university. It aimed to offer to a youth a general cultural education, and to send him out into the world a cultivated man, knowing his mother tongue and some Greek and Latin and mathematics, in touch with literature and science, and with a mind so trained as to enable him to take up a profession or a business with intelligence and success.

There were men in the colleges—Agassiz, Gibbs, Young and others—who were engaged in research, but their researches were in the main personal. The conscious purpose of the college was to teach and, as a teaching agency, to bring the college youth to an understanding and appreciation of the intellectual life—in a word, to teach the boy to think.

In their haste to become universities, our colleges adopted the name and then proceeded as rapidly as possible to grow up to it. This was effected by superimposing a graduate school on the old college. Two disparate educational agencies were merged into one. It was the first great merger.

The graduate students, most of whom are candidates for the doctor's degree in science, literature, education or the professions of law and medicine, have little in common with the youths in the undergraduate college who make up, in most cases, the majority of the whole body of students. But the yoking together of the graduate university and the undergraduate college had a profound effect upon the ideals and methods of the college. The obligation to teach was subordinated to that of research. The college youth now shares the freedom of the man or woman in the graduate school. Teaching as a disciplinary process was considered out of place in a university. College teaching became, more and more, a process of handing out information in all fields of knowledge, rather than a vigorous intellectual experience. Examinations and coaching agencies to help college boys to acquire the necessary credits multiplied amazingly.

The university, as so constituted, soon began to conceive of itself not merely as an agency for training students to think hard and clearly, but as a place where, without fundamental education, young people can acquire the elementary technique of business, banking, accounting, transportation, salesmanship, journalism and, in effect, all the vocations practiced in a modern industrial state. From the exposition of esoteric Buddhism to the management of chain grocery stores, it offers its services to the enquiring young American.

It is under this regime that college sports have been developed from games played by boys for pleasure into systematic professionalized athletic contests for the glory and, too often, for the financial profit of the college. It is important to trace out the process by which this has come about. But such an enquiry is only a section of a much larger one, namely, an evaluation of the intellectual quality of the agency which has suffered such a transformation.

The question is whether an institution in the social order whose primary purpose is the development of the intellectual life can at the same time serve as an agency to promote business, industry, journalism, salesmanship and organized athletics on an extensive commercial basis.

The question is not so much whether athletics in their present form should be fostered by the university, but how fully can a university that fosters professional athletics discharge its primary function. It is true the athletes belong (in recent years) to the college half of the university. Now and again one hears from the graduate school side of the university a protest against the all-absorbing glamour of the athlete, and from the college side a complaint that the graduate students lack college "patriotism." But the fact remains that the same administration that is seeking to promote scholarship and research in the graduate school is responsible for the stadiums, the paid coach and the gate receipts in the college.

How far can an agency, whose function is intellectual, go in the development of other causes without danger to its primary purpose? Can a university teach equally well philosophy and salesmanship? Can it both sponsor genuine education and at the same time train raw recruits for minor vocations? Can it concentrate its attention on securing teams that win, without impairing the sincerity and vigor of its intellectual purpose?

It is to these questions that the thoughtful man is finally led if he seeks to reconcile the divergent activities of the present-day American university. The matter of athletics is only one feature in the picture, but a significant one.

The game of football looms large in any account of the growth of professionalism in college games. This does not mean that other sports are untouched by the influences that have converted football into a professional vocation.

The unfavorable results upon students through the athletic development may be briefly stated in the following terms:

1. The extreme development of competitive games in the colleges has reacted upon the secondary schools. The college athlete begins his athletic career before he gets to college.

2. Once in college the student who goes in for competitive sports, and in particular for football, finds himself under a pressure, hard to resist, to give his whole time and thought to his athletic career. No college boy training for a major team can have much time for thought or study.

3. The college athlete, often a boy from a modest home, finds himself suddenly a most important man in the college life. He begins to live on a scale never before imagined. A special table is provided. Sport clothes and expensive trips are furnished him out of the athletic chest. He jumps at one bound to a plane of living of which he never before knew, all at the expense of some fund of which he knows little. When he drops back to a scale of living such as his own means can afford, the result is sometimes disastrous.

4. He works (for it is work, not play) under paid professional coaches whose business it is to develop the boy to be an effective unit in a team. The coach of today is no doubt a more cultivated man than the coach of twenty years ago. But any father who has listened to the professional coaching a college team will have some misgivings as to the cultural value of the process.

5. Intercollegiate athletics are highly competitive. Every college or university longs for a winning team in its group. The coach is on the alert to bring the most promising athletes in the secondary schools to his college team. A system of recruiting and subsidizing has grown up, under which boys are offered pecuniary and other inducements to enter a particular college. The system is demoralizing and corrupt, alike for the boy who takes the money and for the agent who arranges it, and for the whole group of college and secondary school boys who know about it.

6. Much discussion has been had as to the part the college graduate should have in the government of his college. In the matter of competitive athletics, the college alumnus has, in the main, played a sorry role. It is one thing for an "old grad" to go

back and coach the boys of his college as at Oxford or Cambridge, where there are no professional coaches and no gate receipts. It is quite another thing for an American college graduate to pay money to high school boys, either directly or indirectly, in order to enlist their services for a college team. The process is not only unsportsmanlike, it is immoral to the last degree. The great body of college graduates are wholly innocent in this matter. Most college men wish their college to win. Those who seek to compass that end by recruiting and subsidizing constitute a small, but active, minority, working oftentimes without the knowledge of the college authorities. This constitutes the most disgraceful phase of recent intercollegiate athletics.

7. The relation of organized sports to the health of college students is not a simple question. The information to deal with it completely is not yet at hand. In general it may be said that the relation of college organized sports to the health of the individual student is one dependent on the good sense exhibited by the college boy in participating in such sports, and to the quality of the advice he receives from the college medical officer.

8. For many games, the strict organization and the tendency to commercialize the sport have taken the joy out of the game. In football, for example, great numbers of boys do not play football, as in English schools and colleges, for the fun of it. A few play intensely. The great body of students are onlookers.

9. Finally, it is to be said that the blaze of publicity in which the college athlete lives is a demoralizing influence for the boy himself and no less so for his college.

Appendix II

EXCERPTS FROM AND EXPLANATIONS OF *Bylaws and Interpretations*
OF THE NATIONAL COLLEGIATE ATHLETIC ASSOCIATION

ARTICLE ONE
RECRUITING

Section 1. Contacts and Offers. (A) No member of an institution's athletic staff or other representative of athletic interests shall solicit the enrollment of any prospective student-athlete at his institution by giving or offering to give financial aid or equivalent inducements, except such aid as is permitted by this Association and his institution and the conference of which it may be a member.

O.I. 100. A "student-athlete" is a student whose metriculation was solicited by a member of the athletic staff or other representative of athletic interests with a view toward the student's ultimate participation in the varsity intercollegiate athletic program. Any other student becomes a "student-athlete" only when he reports for a freshman or varsity squad which is under the jurisdiction of the department of intercollegiate athletics. A student is not deemed a "student-athlete" solely because of his prior participation in high school athletics.

(a) A prospective student becomes a prospective "student-athlete" (i.e., matriculation is considered to have been solicited) if a member of the athletic staff or other representative of athletic interests: (1) provides transportation to the prospective student to visit its campus; (2) entertains the prospective student in any way on the campus except the institution may make available to the prospect a complimentary admission to an athletic contest; (3) initiates or arranges a telephone conversation with the prospective student or member of his family (or guardian) for the purpose of recruitment, or (4) entertains members of the family (or guardian) of a prospective student on its campus.

(b) Matriculation is considered not to have been solicited if a member of the athletic staff or other representative of athletic interests: (1) comes in normal contact (without prearrangement) with a prospective student or members of his family (or guardian) and exhibits normal civility excluding any attempts to recruit the prospect or (2) requests via mail a prospective student or a member of his family (or guardian) to complete and return a questionnaire relative to his high school, preparatory school or junior college record.

(B) Any staff member or other representative of a member institution's athletic interests desiring to contact a prospective student-athlete at his high school, college preparatory school or junior college shall first contact that institution's executive officer or his authorized representative, explain the purpose of his call and request permission to contact the student-athlete. Contact may be made at these places only when such permission is granted. No contact with a prospective student-athlete shall be made at the site of his school's athletic competition when the prospect is a participant therein.

O.I. 101. If an institution's staff member requests an alumnus or other friend of the institution to recruit a particular prospect, or has knowledge that the alumnus or friend is recruiting the prospect, then said alumnus or friend becomes a "representative of athletic interests" of that institution. Once a person is identified as a representative, it is presumed he retains that identity.

O.I. 102. The gift of any article of clothing or equipment (including training shirts bearing the institution's identification) to a prospective student-athlete shall be an improper inducement.

O.I. 103. An institution or its representative shall not furnish a prospective student-athlete, either directly or indirectly, with transportation to the campus for his enrollment.

O.I. 104. An institution or its representative shall not offer a prospective student-athlete free transportation to or from a summer job, unless it is the employer's established policy to transport all employees from that locale to the job site.

O.I. 105. "Contact" with a prospect "at the site of his school's athletic competition" (high school, college preparatory school or junior college) shall be governed by the following:

(a) No contact shall be made with such prospect before the competition during the day of the competition.

(b) If the prospect reports on call at the direction of the coach (or comparable authority) and is to be involved in team activity from that point to the end of the competition (e.g., traveling to an away-from-home game) and this occurs prior to the day of competition, then no contact shall be made from the time the prospect reports until after the competition.

(c) After the competition has been completed, the "site" shall be interpreted as the facility in which the competition was conducted and any dressing room or meeting facility utilized in conjunction with the competition. Accordingly, contact shall not be made after the competition at the site until the prospective student-athlete is released by the appropriate institutional authority, he dresses and he departs the dressing and meeting facility.

(d) If a prospective student-athlete is involved in competition which requires his participation more than one day (e.g., basketball tournament) paragraphs (a) and (b) apply and no contact shall be made during the periods between the prospect's competition until his final contest is completed, he is released by the appropriate institutional authority, he dresses and he departs the dressing room or meeting room facility utilized in conjunction with his final participation in the competition.

(C) No member institution shall publicize or arrange publicity of the commitment of a prospective student-athlete to attend the institution or accept its tender of financial assistance other than through its normal media outlets. Press conferences, receptions, dinners or similar meetings held for the purpose of making such announcements are expressly prohibited; further, no member institution shall publicize or arrange publicity of the visit of a prospective student-athlete to the institution's campus. (Revised: 8/1/73)

Section 2. Use of Funds. (A) All funds for the recruiting of prospective student-athletes shall be deposited with the member institution which shall be exclusively and entirely responsible for the manner in which it expends the funds.

(B) No member institution shall permit any outside organization, agency or group of individuals to utilize, administer or expend funds for recruiting prospective student-athletes, including the transportation and entertainment of, and the giving of gifts or services to, prospective student-athletes or their relatives and friends.

(C) The pooling of resources for recruiting purposes by two or more persons shall constitute such a fund; except that this provision shall not apply to persons upon whom a prospective student-athlete may be naturally or legally dependent.

O.I. 106. Bona fide alumni organizations of an institution may sponsor luncheons, teas or dinners at which prospective students (athletes and non-athletes) of that immediate locale are guests.

O.I. 107. (a) A member institution's area alumni organization may be considered a bona fide part of that institution, provided such organization is accredited by the chief executive officer of the institution and meets these additional terms and conditions:

(1) A staff member of the institution periodically shall inspect the financial records of the alumni organization and certify that the expenditures comply with the rules and regulations of the NCAA and the conference of which the institution may be a member.

(2) A club official shall be designated by the chief executive officer as the institution's official agent in the administration of the club's funds, and said club official shall file regular reports to the institution relating the manner in which the club funds have been spent in the recruiting of student-athletes.

(3) To facilitate administration of the one visitation provision of Bylaw 1-5-(a), whenever club funds are used to transport prospective student-athletes to the campus, the club official shall file a report with the institution including the names of the student-athletes so transported.

(b) When an alumni organization is certified by the chief executive officer as being a bona fide part of the institution, said organization becomes subject to all of the limitations placed upon the member institution by NCAA legislation; a violation of such legislation by any member of the alumni organization shall be a violation by the member institution.

O.I. 108. Use of a company's funds to pay the expenses incurred in transporting a prospective student-athlete to his campus constitutes the use of pooled resources.

O.I. 109. A prospective student-athlete may not appear on a radio or television program conducted by the coach of an NCAA member institution, a program in which the coach is participating, or on a program for which a member of the athletic staff of the institution has been instrumental in arranging the prospect's appearance or related program material. This prohibition applies to the prospect's appearance in person or via film or video tape.

Section 3. Tryouts. No member institution shall, on its campus or elsewhere, conduct or have conducted in its behalf any athletic practice session, tryout or test at which one or more prospective student-athletes reveal, demonstrate or display their abilities in any phase of the sport.

O.I. 110. The phrase "prospective student-athletes" shall include any prospect not registered in the institution at the time of the practice or test therein described, except that during preseason practice in fall sports or during practice occurring in mid-year between terms on the academic calendar, it shall be permissible for a student-athlete who is not registered, but who has been accepted for admission to the institution, to engage in such activity provided said practice is not used to determine whether aid is to be awarded.

O.I. 111. The provisions of Bylaw 1-3 shall not apply to:

(a) Developmental clinics or competition involving prospective student-athletes, provided such activity is approved by the NCAA Council and provided the activity is conducted by and subject to the control of the host NCAA member institution.

(b) Regularly scheduled high school athletic contests or matches held on the campus of a member institution, provided the competition is approved by the appropriate state high school authority, or conducted by a national sports federation of which this Association is a member.

(c) The regular or emergency use of a college facility by a high school athletic team for its normal practice activities conducted solely by the high school coaches.

O.I. 112. No member of an institution's coaching staff may conduct or participate in any coaching school or specialized sports camp involving a student who is eligible for admission to a member institution or who has started classes for his senior year in high school.

O.I. 113. A member institution, through its regular team physician or other designated physician, may conduct a medical examination of a prospective student-athlete at the time of his visit to the campus to determine his medical qualifications to participate in intercollegiate athletics, provided the examination is conducted without the presence of any athletic department staff member and it does not include any test or procedure designed to measure the athletic agility or the athletic skills of the prospect.

Section 4. High School All-Star Games. No member institution shall permit any employee to participate, directly or indirectly, in the management, coaching, officiating, supervision, promotion or player selection of any all-star team or contest in football or basketball involving interscholastic players or those who, during the previous school year, were members of high school teams. Facilities of a member institution shall not be made available unless such a contest is first sanctioned by the appropriate state high school athletic association or, if interstate, by the National Federation of State High School Athletic Associations.

O.I. 114. If a coach has made a contractual commitment to coach in a high school all-star game prior to being employed by a member institution, and then becomes a member of the institution's staff before the game is held, the coach shall be obligated to observe this provision and disassociate himself from the all-star game.

Section 5. Transportation, Visitations and Entertainment. (A) A member institution may finance one and only one visit to its campus for a given prospective student-athlete. Such visit shall not exceed forty-eight hours. Only actual round-trip transportation costs by direct route between the student's home and the institution's campus may be paid.

(B) Any person, at his own expense, may transport or pay the transportation costs of a prospective student-athlete to visit the campus of a member institution one time provided such person, at his own expense, accompanies the prospective student-athlete on his visit. Only actual round-trip transportation costs by direct route between the student-athlete's home and the institution's campus may be provided. Such visit shall not exceed forty-eight hours. (Revised: 8/1/74)

(C) No member institution shall permit more than one expense-paid visit to its campus under the authorization of Bylaws 1-5 (a) and (b). A prospective student-athlete may not be provided an expense-paid visit earlier than the opening day of classes of his senior year in school. (Revised: 8/1/72)

(D) No member institution shall permit its athletic staff members or other representatives of its athletic interests to pay or arrange for the payment of the transportation costs incurred by relatives or friends of a prospective student-athlete to visit the campus or elsewhere.

(1) This prohibition shall not apply when a prospective student-athlete travels in an automobile to visit the institution's campus, in which case the institution is permitted to pay the round-trip expense at the same mileage rate it allows for travel by its own personnel even though relatives or friends of the prospect accompany him in the automobile. The automobile cannot be owned, operated or its use arranged by the institution or any representative of its athletic interests. This shall count as a paid visit for each prospective student-athlete who makes the trip. (Revised: 8/1/73)

(2) No member institution shall permit a representative of its athletic interests to transport the relatives or friends of a prospective student-athlete to visit the campus or elsewhere in his own vehicle. Such representative may not pay the commercial transportation costs of a campus visit by the relatives or friends of a prospective student-athlete. (Revised: 8/1/72)

(3) In all instances, entertainment of the party accompanying a prospective student-athlete to the campus shall be limited to his parent (or legal guardian), and a given prospect's parents (or legal guardians) may be entertained for one and only one visit. Such visit shall not exceed forty-eight hours. (Revised: 8/1/73)

(E) An institution, or representative of its athletic interest, may provide entertainment for a prospective student-athlete, his parents (or legal guardians) at the institution's campus only. Transporting a prospective student-athlete to any other site for any purpose is not permissible. Further, it is not permissible to entertain other relatives or friends of a prospective student-athlete at any site. A prospective student-athlete visiting a member institution's campus shall live and take his meals as regular students normally do. If campus facilities are not available, local commercial facilities may be used, but at a scale comparable to that of normal student life. His entertainment shall take place on campus; however, if on-campus entertainment is not available and it is necessary to entertain a prospective student-athlete off-campus, a student host may be provided with a maximum of $10 for each day of the visit to cover the cost of actual and necessary entertainment expenses. No member institution may arrange for or permit excessive entertainment of any prospective student-athlete on the campus or elsewhere. The institution (or representatives of its athletic interests) shall not provide an automobile for the use of the prospect or a student host. (Revised: 8/1/73)

(F) A member institution's athletic staff member or other representative of its athletic interests may visit a prospective student-athlete or his relatives at any location for recruiting purposes. However, on any such visit, neither the staff member (nor any representative of the institution) may expend any funds other than necessary for his own personal expenses. (Adopted: 8/1/72)

(G) If an institution is required to play all of its home games of a given sport at a site located in a community other than its own because of conditions beyond its control (e.g., fire, windstorm, earthquake or other disaster), the institution may apply to the Council or the officers of the Association for permission to consider the substitute site as its home site. Upon approval by the Council or the officers, such games on the substitute site shall be considered on-campus competition.

(H) An institution shall not pay any costs incurred by an athletic talent scout or a representative of its athletic interests in studying or recruiting prospective student-athletes. An institution may not place any such person on a fee or honorarium basis and thereby claim him as a staff member entitled to expense money. (Revised: 8/1/74)

(I) A member institution may entertain high school, college preparatory school or junior college coaches only on its campus or in the community in which the institution is located. Such entertainment may include providing a maximum of two complimentary tickets to home athletic contests, food and refreshments, but shall not include room expenses or the cost of transportation to and from the institution. (Adopted: 8/1/73, Revised: 8/1/74)

O.I. 115. If an institution is to pay the transportation costs of a prospective student-athlete to visit the campus, the visit actually must be made to the campus and not, for example, to some off-campus site where the institution happens to be appearing in an athletic contest at the particular time.

O.I. 116. An institution may not use its own automobile or airplane to transport a prospective student-athlete to the campus if his relatives or other friends accompany him.

O.I. 117. It shall not be permissible for a member institution's athletic staff member, at institutional expense, to drive his own automobile to transport a prospective student-athlete to the campus if the prospect's relatives or friends accompany him. It shall not be permissible for an institution to reimburse a high school, preparatory school or junior college coach for expenses incurred in transporting a prospect to visit the campus.

O.I. 118. Whenever an aircraft (other than a commercial airplane or one owned personally by one individual) is used to transport a prospective student-athlete, payment for its use must be at the established charter rates at the airport where the craft is based, and the institution must be prepared to demonstrate satisfactorily that such payment has been made.

O.I. 127. The NCAA Council has approved an exception to Bylaw 1-6 in regard to the preparatory education programs of the U.S. Air Force, Military and Naval Academies. This action provides that a nonprofit, outside organization representing the interest of one of the academies may collect contributions from alumni and other friends of the academy for the purpose of assisting candidates in obtaining a preparatory education provided that:

(a) The foundation's arrangements with the preparatory school or schools shall provide that the foundation's contributions shall be turned over to the preparatory school for the school's administration without interference or dictation from the foundation or the academy;

(b) The preparatory school shall have sole jurisdiction in determining the recipient of financial assistance and the terms and conditions of the award;

(c) The foundation may recommend candidates to the preparatory school; athletic staff members of the academy may not;

(d) Such a foundation shall provide preparatory education assistance for prospective candidates who do not have specialized athletic abilities as well as those who do. The number of candidates with recognized ability and the number of candidates without such ability assisted each year as the result of the foundation's program shall be in equal ratio to the number of student-athletes on the regular intercollegiate squads of the academy compared to the total enrollment of the academy.

Section 7. College Enrollees. No member of an institution's athletic staff or other representative of its athletic interests shall contact, either directly or indirectly, the student-athlete of another senior collegiate institution for purposes of recruiting him without first obtaining the permission of the other institution's athletic director to do so, regardless of who makes the initial contact.

O.I. 128. If a known student-athlete proposes to transfer from a four-year collegiate institution to another four-year institution holding N.C.A.A. membership, and the first institution declines to give the permission required by Bylaw 1-7, the second institution may not encourage the transfer and may not offer or provide financial assistance to the student-athlete. If the student-athlete proceeds to transfer to the second institution, and the specified permission is not forthcoming, the second institution may not provide the transferee financial aid until he has attended the institution one academic year

O.I. 129. Freshmen (plebes) entering the official summer enrollment program of one of the four national service academies (i.e., U.S. Air Force, Coast Guard, Military and Naval Academies) shall be considered student-athletes of a senior collegiate institution for purposes of Bylaw 1-7, but shall not be considered transfer students (insofar as NCAA legislation is concerned) if at the conclusion of said summer program they shall enroll in another collegiate institution.

Section 8. Specialized Sports Camps, Coaching Schools and Clinics. In operating a specialized sports camp, coaching school or sports clinic, a member institution, members of its staff or representatives of its athletic interests shall not employ or give free or reduced admission privileges to a high school or junior college athletic award winner. (Adopted: 1/13/73)

*   *   *

Article One of the *Bylaws and Interpretations* of the National Collegiate Athletic Association is devoted to the question of recruiting. Following is a paraphrasing of some of the key rules of that Article, together with the author's reasons for the adoption of each of them:

Rule: A student-athlete may not be offered more than a scholarship for room, board, tuition, books and equipment, plus $15 a month. Colleges may, and do, give less.

Reason: To prevent inducements that in the past have ranged from suits of clothes to automobiles and expensive, off-campus apartments. This is considered the most serious regulation on re-cruiting, since it involves violations that could amount to thou-sands of dollars for individual athletes.

Rule: A College may pay for just one visit to its campus by an athlete being recruited. This visit may last only forty-eight hours, during which time a boy must be quartered in a dormitory or comparable living quarters and must be given meals comparable to those offered to undergraduate students on campus. This visit is limited to an athlete's senior year in high school.

Reason: To avoid "hiding" an athlete from other colleges by keeping him on one campus each weekend until he makes his final decision, and to avoid treating him better than other students.

Rule: Coaches and other recruiters may visit a boy as many times as they wish at any location off campus, but they may not pay for the athlete's transportation to any meeting place or spend any money entertaining or feeding him off campus. They may not even buy the athlete "a cup of coffee" off campus.

Reason: To eliminate the old practice of taking a boy to a resort where he might be wined and dined at great expense.

Rule: Any entertainment for a prospective athlete must be provided on the campus, and it must be the recreation or enter-tainment normally provided for students.

Reason: To eliminate expensive wining and dining off cam-pus, and to restrict any entertaining to more or less normal campus levels.

Rule: While on the campus, a recruit may not be provided with an automobile for his own use. Coaches or other officials may drive him around. If a host student serves as a chaperone, that student may drive the athlete only if the host uses his own car. No car may be provided for the student chaperone.

Reason: To offer only the type of transportation a student might expect once he enrolls at a college.

Rule: A coach or recruiter may not talk to a prospective athlete on the day of his competition in any high-school sports event until after the game is over, and then only after the coach or recruiter has obtained the permission of the athlete's coach or supervisor. In the case of a tournament lasting more than one day, a college recruiter may not approach the athlete until after his final competition in the tournament.

Reason: To cut down on the interruption of an athlete's participation in any high-school event and to provide equal chances for recruiters to reach athletes with personal contacts.

Rule: A college may not provide free transportation, gifts, or entertainment off campus to any relative or friend of the athlete.

Reason: To prevent inducements to parents and others who may have an important influence on the athlete.

Rule: At no time may a college coach or recruiter test the athletic skills of a student-athlete with such things as time trials, practice games, weight drills, basket shooting, blocking or tackling drills, etc. The recruiter may, however, watch the boy in high-school games that are a regular part of his secondary-school team requirements.

Reason: To take away the added pressure of forcing a boy to "make the college team" before even getting the scholarship, and to eliminate offers to a recruit based on his accomplishments within a controlled environment.

Index

About the Author

Joseph Durso, a sports writer for *The New York Times*, has been with the paper since 1950, and has seen duty as a metropolitan news editor and as assistant to the national news editor. The author of seven books on sports, Mr. Durso has written for most major magazines, is on the faculty of Columbia University's Graduate School of Journalism, and has broadcast in New York for WQXR and the Public Broadcasting System. A pilot in the U.S. Air Force in World War II, he graduated *magna cum laude* from New York University in 1946, and was elected to Phi Beta Kappa, and earned a master's degree from Columbia University the following year.